Old Halifax, Sowerby Ripponden and Rishworth

Phil Sunderland

A view in Ripponden down Elland Road, which dips into the Ryburn Valley and rises steeply again leading to Barkisland, Norland, Stainland, Greetland and Elland. The chimney and tower above the shops belong to Chapel Field Mill. On the left amongst the trees is the Vicarage. The building with two gables between the trees and the chimney is Ripponden school. Above the school is Ripponden and Barkisland Station. The bridge carrying the track to Rishworth can also be seen.

Stenlake Publishing Ltd

First Published in the United Kingdom, 2015
by Stenlake Publishing Limited
54-58 Mill Square, Catrine, KA5 6RD
www.stenlake.co.uk

Printed by
Blissetts, E1 – 8 Shield Drive, West Cross Industrial Park, Brentford, TW8 9EX

ISBN 9781840336696

TOWN HALL, SOWERBY BRIDGE.

The horse and cart are crossing County Bridge, heading towards Triangle. The bridge crosses the River Calder and a few yards downstream is joined by the Ryburn. Also known as Town End Bridge, it was first mentioned in 1314 when the township was fined for failing to keep the bridge in good repair. The first stone bridge was built in 1517 and widened in 1632. In 1644, during the Civil War, the Battle of Sowerby Bridge was fought to capture the bridge – the Royalists were defending it but were defeated by the Parliamentary forces. In 1673 it became known as the County Bridge. Daniel Defoe passed through the area on his travels around England in 1725 and described the bridge as a 'stately structure of several stone arches'. The bridge was widened in 1733, 1821 and 1875, and in 1925 it was placed on the list of scheduled monuments.

Acknowledgements

The author would like to thank the following for their assistance while writing this book: John and Doreen Wadsworth, Donald Taylor and Stephen Gee.

Further Reading

The books listed below were used by the author during his research. None of them is available from Stenlake Publishing. Those interested in finding out more are advised to contact their local bookshop or reference library.

Ripponden History Guide
Sowerby Bridge, David Cliff
The Rishworth Branch, Jeffrey N. Fisher
Halifax History Tour, Stephen Gee

Halifax Rugby Club the first 100 Years, Andrew Hardcastle
Halifax Town the Complete Record, Johnny Meyneil
History of Rishworth School, J.H. Priestley
Martin Bull's Calderdale Companion website.

Halifax

Halifax is on the eastern slopes of the Pennines, approximately seven miles south-west of Bradford, seventeen miles south-west of Leeds, 22 miles north-east of Manchester and 194 miles north of London. It is centrally placed in the country as it is 65 miles to Kingston-upon-Hull on the Yorkshire coast and the same distance to Liverpool on the Lancashire coast. The town covers 75,000 acres and according to the 2011 census had a population of 88,134.

The name Halifax is first recorded in 1091, with a variation in the spelling – 'Halyfax'. There are several ideas as to where the name came from, probably the corruption of the Old English words 'Hay' and 'Ley', with 'Hay' meaning a clearing or meadow. Haley or Hayley are common surnames in the area and there is a hamlet called Healey and also a Haley hill. There is no mention of the town in the Domesday Book, but by the twelfth century it had become the religious centre for the massive parish of Halifax, extending from Brighouse in the east to Heptonstall in the west. In 1677 William Savile became the first Viscount Halifax, and later became Marquess of Halifax. George Montagu-Dunk, the second Earl of Halifax became president of the Board of Trade in 1748 and the following year helped to found the town (later city) of Halifax, the capital of Nova Scotia. He also gave his name to the Halifax River in Central Florida.

Cloth manufacturing was always the main employer in the Halifax area. Originally weavers would work in their cottages and trade their goods at the cloth markets in the town. Many of the older cottages in the area have upstairs windows that cover the full length of the building these were to allow as much light as possible into the room to help the weaver. As the industry became mechanised these home weavers had to move into the mills that were springing up alongside the rivers all over the area. Eventually, the industry gave rise to J. Crossley & Son, in the nineteenth century the biggest carpet manufacturer in the world. Halifax was also the home of two other world-famous companies. In 1892 recently married Violet Macintosh was selling homemade cakes, pastries and tarts from a small rented shop at 53 King Cross Street. She devised a recipe to combine traditional English brittle toffee with the softer caramel that was being imported from America and called this Mackintosh's Celebrated Toffee, a big hit with the locals. Within seven years, and several premises, each one bigger than the last, the company became John Mackintosh Ltd (John was her husband). In 1932 it started to make chocolate, creating the brands Milk Tray and Quality Street. Other favourites followed: Rolo in 1937 and Toffee Crisp in 1963 to name just a couple. In 1969 the company merged with York-based Rowntrees and became Rowntree Mackintosh (the Mackintosh was dropped in 1987). The company was taken over by Nestle in June 1988 at a cost of £2.25 billion.

The third major company to be born in Halifax is the building society. In March 1921 the Halifax Permanent Building Society took over a purpose-built department store on Commercial Street as its headquarters. In 1928 there was a merger between the Halifax Permanent Building Societies of 1853 and 1900 and the Halifax Equitable Building Society, to form the Halifax Building Society. In the 1970s new premises were built in Trinity Road on the site of the old Ramsden's Stone Trough Brewery. In 1997 the society became a bank and in 2001 merged with the Bank of Scotland.

Another famous Halifax brand was Samuel Webster's beer, which he began brewing in 1838 at his Fountain Head Brewery. In 1892 the firm recorded net profits for the year at the present day equivalent of £2 million. Just over one hundred years later, the brewery closed in 1996 with the loss of 400 jobs. Its most famous brews were Green label, Pennine Bitter and a bottled brown ale called Sam Brown.

Halifax has also produced its fair share of high achievers, including Percy Shaw, inventor of the cat's eye, Phyllis Bentley the novelist, the actors Eric Portman and Wilfred Pickles, the judge James Pickles, John Tillotson, Archbishop of Canterbury in the 1690s, the TV presenter John Noakes, and the singer Ed Sheeran to name but a few.

PHONE :- 4668

LIGHT LORRIES
AND
VANS FOR HIRE

A. ROBERTS

LIGHT HAULAGE CONTRACTOR
AND DELIVERY SPECIALIST
12, NORTH PARADE, HALIFAX

LOCAL DELIVERY.
SERVICES, ALSO
DAILY PARCEL SERVICE
TO ALL PARTS OF
LANCASHIRE

A. Roberts was one of many firms in the Halifax area bidding for business of transferring goods to and from Lancashire. Probably the biggest of these companies was Ripponden & District which were based midway between Ripponden and Rishworth. The decline of the mills and the introduction of supermarkets saw the end of most of these carriers.

Halifax Tram No. 86 on its way through Skircoat Green. On 1 July 1906 a tram descending New Bank on its way into the town ran out of control and overturned at North Bridge. Luckily, it was 7.30 on a Sunday morning and there were only fifteen passengers, although two were killed and a further nine were taken to Halifax Infirmary. One of the victims was Arthur Rushworth, 24, and the other was an itinerant Irish labourer who was in the area to work on the harvest. Nobody knew who he was, but five women came forward to claim compensation for the death of her husband. The driver, Theodore Chadwick, was sacked over the incident, judged to have applied the brakes incorrectly on the damp slippery rails. He was cleared by an inquest but the tram company refused to reinstate him. This caused a strike amongst the tram drivers and, on 31 August, 20 drivers were imported from Bristol to ease the situation. By 5 September a 13,000-signature petition had been handed to the town council asking them to sort out the situation: within the next ten days 40 drivers had returned to work and the strike was over.

Ogden Old Mill. Ogden is an area to the north of the town centre, heading towards Keighley. Right of centre can be seen the mill pond. This water would have been drawn from a local stream, kept in a confined area in order to provide a constant source of water power for the mill.

The Halifax Gibbet or guillotine was used for public executions from the thirteenth to the seventeenth centuries. A commission set up by Edward I in 1278 reported that there were 94 privately owned gibbets and gallows in Yorkshire, but the gibbet at Halifax was used after all the rest had long disappeared. The last two men to be beheaded were Abraham Wilkinson, who stole sixteen yards of cloth, and Anthony Mitchell, who thieved two horses. They were both caught, tried and executed on the same day, 30 April 1650. Records were not kept until the parish registers began in 1538 so the total number of people executed in Halifax will never be known. It is recorded that from 1538 there were 56 men and women beheaded. John of Dalton was most likely to have been the first victim in 1286 and it is thought that there could have been almost 100 executions in total. Gibbet law said that if the person could retract their head before being struck by the blade and make it across the River Hebble they could be freed. There are no recorded instances of this! The base seen here was discovered in 1840 and is now a listed building. The original blade is in Bankfield Museum.

Bull Green, as it used to be. It is totally unrecognisable today. The road leading of to the right under the far tram pole is George Street; it was partially demolished and widened in the late 1930s, probably over 30 years after this photo was taken. The road where the photographer is standing leads out of the town through King Cross and on to the Ryburn and Calder valleys.

Skircoat Moor Road passes over the moor which is situated east of the Crossley Heath School in King Cross on the outskirts of Halifax. The school was built in 1863 with funding from John, Joseph and Francis Crossley and opened as the Crossley Orphanage. Thomas Porter made a donation to the project in 1887 and the name changed to the Crossley and Porter Orphanage. In 1919 it became a school and in 1985 amalgamated with near neighbours Heath School to become Crossley Heath School. The moor, which was originally farmland, is about 63 acres in total, and has been used for a variety of purposes over the years. In 1478 there was a skirmish here between the combined forces of the Saviles and Stansfields against the Pilkingtons. The Saviles were from Halifax, the Stansfields from Wadsworth, which is high in the hills above Hebden Bridge, and the Pilkingtons from Skipton in Craven. These families had been feuding for years with indictments going back to 1460 and involving livestock theft, assault, damage, extortion, imprisonment for ransom, and murder. This all culminated on Skircoat Moor on 19 May 1478 with the skirmish that resulted in at least eight deaths. The moor was used to hold public meetings by organisations such as the Chartists and the so-called 'Plug Rioters'. These were mill workers who were worried about steam power coming to the mills and threatening their jobs. They travelled the area of Halifax and Bradford gaining access to the mills by force, removing the plugs from the boilers and emptying the water from the mill dams, causing the mills to stop production until repairs had been made. They held a large meeting on the moor on 15 August 1842 and then marched into Halifax to Akroyd's Power Loom Shed. They were met at the mill by soldiers who opened fire on the rioters, killing one and wounding several others. In 1886 the land was bought by Henry Savile who turned it into a public park, with the stipulation that it should never be fenced. Other uses for the park have included horse racing in the 1730s and, in more recent times, it has become the home of the annual Halifax Show.

Spring Hall, Skircoat, Huddersfield Road, Halifax. The present building was built in 1871 as a home for Tom Holdsworth, a local businessman. In May 1881 he was attending an auction at Christies & Mansons in London and was found dead in his hotel bedroom. The next occupant was also a Holdsworth, probably his son. In the 1890s the site was bought by the Midland Railway Company with a view to turning it into a goods yard but this idea was abandoned. From 1 February 1916 to 28 February 1918 the property was taken over as a hospital for wounded soldiers, providing 84 beds, with an annex added in April 1917. After the war in 1919 J.H. Whitley bought the house to use as a guest house for his business associates and in

May 1920 he offered the house as a guest house for young men. This closed in 1931 and until 1938 it remained unoccupied. Paton & Baldwin, knitting yarn and pattern producers, bought the place in 1938 and, after use as a hospital in the Second World War, in 1948 presented it to the town, with the official handover being performed by Princess Elizabeth and the Duke of Edinburgh in July 1949. The site later became a sports venue and was used annually for the school sports for all the grammar schools in the Ryburn and Calder valleys. In 1990 it was briefly the home of the Northern Ballet Theatre Company, and it is now owned by the Calderdale Council and can be used as a wedding venue.

A peaceful scene along Moor Lane, Illingworth. This area is to the north of the town centre on the route to Keighley. It was in the Township of Ovenden before being incorporated into the Borough of Halifax. Since the 1950s several housing estates have been built here there are few views left similar to this one. A tram link with Halifax was established in the last months of the nineteenth century, opening on 5 August 1899. Illingworth St. Mary's Cricket Club was founded here in 1884, named after the local church which dates back to 1525. The land for the original church was given by Henry Saville, Lord of the Manor of Ovenden. This was one acre of waste land for the purpose of building a free church to honour the Blessed Virgin Mary, but in return he or his heirs were to receive a red rose each year as a rent. This might seem as though the land was being given away but this agreement was binding, and failure to provide the bloom would forfeit the land back to the lord of the manor. The arrangement was common practice at that time. In 1777 a new church was built at a cost of £1,400 with improvements being added at various times, including an organ in 1807 and a safe in 1818. Nothing is sacred however as this safe was stolen, opened, emptied and dumped in a quarry behind the church. A memorial to Privates E. Atkinson and J.W. Drake, lost in the First World War, is at the church. It was carved by Harry Percy Jackson

Boothtown Road, leading out of Halifax, looks here to be a good, flat, easily navigable road, but part of it is at a gradient of 1 in 9.7 which caused problems when the tramway company were planning new routes from the town. The original road was widened in 1930. On the left of the photo is Akroyd Park Lodge. This was bought by Halifax Town Council from Edward Akroyd in November 1886 for £6,000. In 1887 Akroyd died and the park, including the mansion and eight acres of park land became known as Akroyd Park. On the right side of the photo is Woodside Baths which

were originally to have been built in the park. They consisted of a swimming pool, 16 slipper baths and a public laundry, and opened to the public on 6 July 1893. The building became unsafe in 1920 and was closed for a major overhaul, and during the Second World War it was used as a first aid station. It was finally closed in 1982 and was demolished in 1985. The other major feature in the photo is All Souls Church, originally known as All Souls Haley Hill. The first stone was laid here on 25 April 1856, and the church was consecrated on 2 November 1859.

Hall End is at the top of Crown Street and Silver Street. A cloth market hall was mentioned here as early as 1572 and it went by several different names, including Blackwell Hall. The hall was rebuilt about 1700 and called the Linen Hall. It was demolished in 1820 when the area was redeveloped and Waterhouse Street came into being. In the eighteenth century Crown Street had been a narrow street, only about fourteen feet wide with the upper stories of the properties reaching out over the street. In July 1886 the Town Council purchased the street and demolished the majority of it to widen the road. The new buildings are therefore Victorian, except for one property, No. 11, which is known to have been there since 1733. Silver Street was similarly redeveloped, although slightly earlier in 1882.

Right: On 30 October 1937 King George VI and Queen Elizabeth were welcomed into Halifax by a 21-gun salute fired from Beacon Hill. They are pictured here with the mayor, Councillor C. Hodgson J.P. The royal couple took lunch at Shibden Hall, before visiting Elland and Brighouse. This was their first visit to the area.

Below: The road leading out through Ovenden on its way to Illingworth, Haworth and Keighley was built in 1880. To construct the road it meant knocking down part of Watkinson Hall which had been built in 1783. It had been used as a cloth warehouse and many generations of the Watkinson family had lived there. Along with Illingworth, Ovenden had been used in the second half of the 1900s to provide housing on a large scale, so this quiet scene is unimaginable now. In more recent times Ovenden has been the home of Halifax Rugby Union Club. This was formed in 1919 and used several grounds before settling at Ovenden Park in 1928. They initially rented the ground for £1 per year, until local businessman Jack Standeven bought the ground. This passed onto his sons, who in 1950 presented the ground to the club in memory of their father. The club holds a record thirteen Yorkshire Cup Final victories, including three won consecutively in 1926, 1927 and 1928. Seventy club members have represented Yorkshire, and four have represented their country. Harry Wilkinson played four internationals between 1929–30, Phillip Horrocks-Taylor nine between 1958–64, and Lt. Col. Charles Kirke Tindall Faithfull, known as 'Chubby', played three times between 1924–1926. Michael Campbell Lammerton represented Scotland on 23 occasions between 1961 and 1966 and also toured and captained the British Lions. In the modern era Richard Szabro won two caps for Hungary in 2004–2005.

OVN. 6   TOP BEECHWOOD ROAD, OVENDEN

A view from Wards End along Southgate, with the spire of the Town Hall in the distance. The building on the left with the canopy is the Palace Theatre. This was officially opened on 30 July 1903, with the first public performance four days later. The stone laying ceremony was performed by Mayor William Brear on 4 October 1902. Across the street the other building with a canopy is the Theatre Royal. This was built on the site of an old theatre and opened on the 4 August 1905. It cost £40,000 to build.

Bermerside, Skircoat, Halifax. The first house on this site was Skircoat House which was built for William Newby, a local merchant, in the eighteenth century. George Haigh was the second owner of the house and he changed its name to Bermerside, taking the name from a poem written by Thomas the Rhymer, 'Tyde what may betyde, Haigh shall be laird of Bermerside'. Haigh lived from 1763 to 1849. The third occupants were three Rawson sisters who renamed the house Ravenscliffe. When one of the sisters married all three moved out. Edward Crossley bought the house, knocked it down and built the house seen here, calling it Bermerside. On 20 July 1908 Bermerside Convalescent Home and School was opened, better known as Bermerside open air school. This was one of three sites around the town linked with the education of children with special requirements. The plan of the school was to provide the children with fresh air, good food, exercise and medical attention.

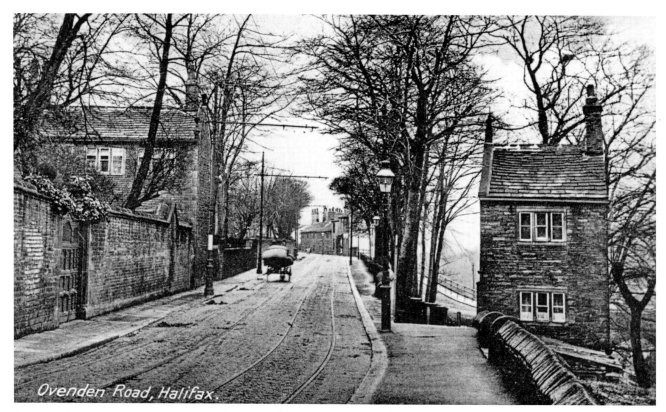

Ovenden Road, looking in the direction of Ovenden. The building behind the wall to the left of the road is Ovenden Hall. There is mention of this house in the sixteenth century, but the present house is the second one on the site, built by Joseph Fourness in 1662. Fourness (1603–1667) made his money as a cloth seller and manufacturers' agent at the Blackwell Hall in London, a specialist cloth market. He also owned Upper Shibden Hall and Calico Hall in Halifax. He took the Parliamentary side in the Civil War. Refurbishment was undertaken by Gamaleil Sutcliffe, probably around 1800. There is no date for this work but Sutcliffe lived from 1750–1840. By 1944 the hall was a home for the local elderly and in 1945 was taken over by Miss Jane Carter. She lived there for 21 years until her death in 1966 aged 103.

After the Poor Law Amendment Act of 1834 every town in the country built a workhouse. This building was part of the Halifax workhouse which opened on 25 March 1840. It was built on a site between Gibbet Street and Hanson Lane and went by several names: Halifax Poor Law Institute, Gibbet Street Institute and Halifax Union Workhouse and Hospital. Later, by 1891, it was also called St John's Hospital. In 1901 a new hospital was built at Salterhebble to ease the overcrowding here by taking away the bedridden patients. The building was used as an auxiliary hospital during the First World War and it has since been demolished.

A view along Commercial Street, taken from Hall End. This is the main street and it was a popular drop off point for trams. The shop to the right of the tram is advertising fine leather goods and above is one of Webster's cafés. G. Webster & Son was founded in 1819, with a first property in Crown Street. 1825 saw a move to Silver Street, and other branches were opened around the town and other areas along the Calder and Ryburn valleys. The Imperial in George Street was a very popular branch and became the place to be seen taking tea or coffee. After the Second World War the business began to suffer and the two main cafés in the town centre, the Imperial and the Mikado, which had been opened in 1889, were closed. Branches in Hebden Bridge, Hipperholme, King Cross and Salterhebble followed, as did the bakery in Mount Street, Halifax. Webster's ceased trading in 1963 after almost 150 years.

The Electric Theatre at Sunny Vale Pleasure Gardens, Hipperholme, a couple of miles east of Halifax. This was opened on 1 May 1880 by Joseph Bunce. Joseph lived at a nearby farm and in the summer months would provide a table of tea and cakes for Sunday walkers as they passed by. He saw a future in this venture and bought the land in the valley, providing attractions to entice visitors. There were two lakes on which he provided steam boat rides and other attractions included a dining room, maze, music, shows, carnivals, swings, helter skelter, skating and dancing. The Electric Theatre seen here is probably the Palace of Illusions which Bunce bought from the Bradford Exhibition. At one point the site was attracting almost 100,000 customers

per year and more land was purchased to provide the space. The entrance fee was 1d; a bulk buy of 24 tickets was 18d. The dining room was equipped to feed 1,000 people but in the good years was providing food for 4,000 most Saturdays. A small gauge railway was introduced in 1916, bought from Halifax Zoo which closed that year. The engine was known as Baby Bunce. 1912 saw a re-enactment of the Titanic disaster at the park, and at the end of each season there was a big firework display. On 24 August 1940 a German bomber, trying to avoid searchlights, dropped seven bombs on the site. This caused little damage but a nearby farmer charged 10d for allowing people to cross his land to view the craters, the profits going to the Red Cross. The park was sold in 1945 and closed in 1949. In 1958 the park was sold again, to Bert Myers who renamed it Sunny Vale Country Club. In the 1960s and 70s it was used for go-kart and stock car racing, but gradually fell into disrepair.

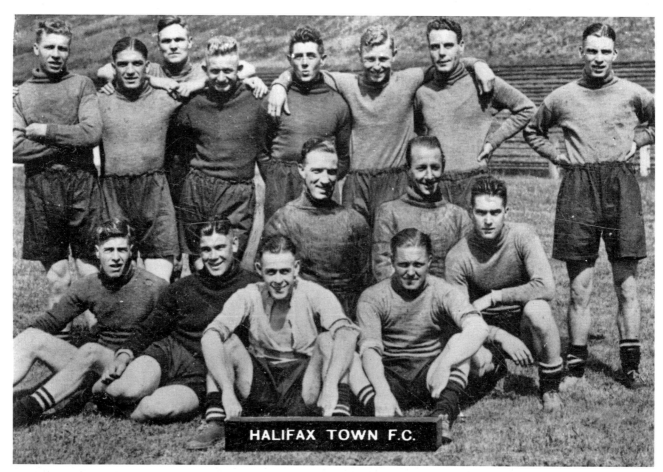

HALIFAX TOWN F.C.

Halifax Town Football Club was formed on 23 May 1911 at a meeting at the Saddle Hotel, Halifax. The first games were played at the Sandhall Lane ground and 1919 saw a move to Exley, the former ground of Salterhebble Rugby Union Club. Finally, in 1921 the club moved to the Shay ground at Shaw Hill. The first game at the Shay attracted more than 10,000 and saw the home team beat Darlington 5–1. In 1921 the club achieved football league status. This is the 1934–35 team, runners-up in the Third Division – Northern Section that season.

Back row, left to right: C. Smethurst, C. Smith, W. Allsop, A. Valentine, F. Tunstall, G. Millington, A. Hale and C. Davies.

Middle row, left to right: I. Williams and C. Owen.

Front row, left to right: J. Coode, A. Pope, T. Barkas, T. Fleeney and F. Betteridge.

T. S. LANGFORD

542 HALIFAX TOWN

Tom Langford was born in Wolverhampton on 4 October 1892. He came from Swindon Town to play for Halifax Town for the 1922–23 season and made 29 appearances without scoring. He died in 1960.

16

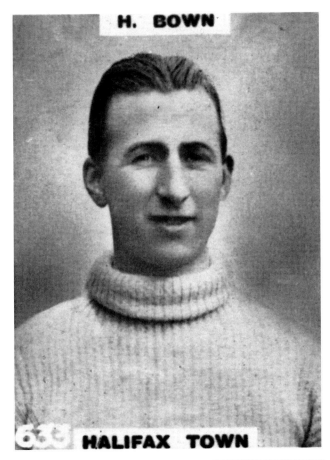

H. BOWN

HALIFAX TOWN

M. F. ELLSON

HALIFAX TOWN

M. WELLOCK

Herbert Bown was a goalkeeper who joined Halifax Town for the start of the 1922–23 season from Leicester City. He played at the Shay for two seasons and did not miss a match, playing 93 consecutive games. At the end of the 1923–24 season he moved on to Hull City. On 5 May 1923, in a home Third Division North game against Stalybride Celtic, he scored a penalty in the 2–1 victory. This was the last day of the season and Town finished seventh in their second season in the football league. They also reached the first round of the FA Cup after three qualifying rounds, but lost 3–1 to South Shields in the first round proper.

Merton Ellson was born in Thropston, Northamptonshire, on 10 July 1893. He joined Halifax Town from Frickley Colliery in 1922. He played for two seasons, making 27 appearances in the football league and FA Cup, scoring six goals. In a Third Division North game at Tranmere Rovers on 30 September 1922 he was sent off for retaliation.

Maurice Wellock joined Halifax Town in 1919 whilst they were playing in the Midland Counties League. In the 1919–20 and 1920–21 seasons he played in 53 matches and scored seven goals. Halifax Town joined the football league the following season and he was retained. He played in 32 games that season, scoring three goals. The following season he made just one appearance before moving on. In his career he also played for Bradford City, Darlington and Blackpool. He returned to the Shay for the 1932–33 and 1933–34 seasons. In total at Halifax he played in 126 games and scored 28 times in the football league. On 22 April 1922, in a Division Three North game at Chesterfield, he committed a bad foul towards the end of the game and was sent from the field.

F. DENT

G. H. WILD

Fred Dent was born on 24 January 1896 and played two seasons at Halifax Town: 1921–22 and 1922–23. He made 39 appearances and scored thirteen goals. He arrived via Sheffield Wednesday and was transferred to Chesterfield. He died in 1995, aged 99. Halifax Town joined the football league in the Third Division North in season 1921–22, with a best return of second in 1934–35. In 1958–59 the Third Division North changed to the Third Division proper and in 1962–63 Town finished bottom and were relegated to Division Four. 1968–69 saw them finish second and gain promotion, with third place coming in 1970–71. 1975–76 was a bad year and again the team was relegated to Division Four. This was later followed by relegation to the Conference in 1992–93. Promotion in 1997–98 to the new Division Three of the Football League lasted just five seasons with relegation once again to the Conference.

George Wild was a Sowerby Bridge lad, born on 30 September 1887. He joined Halifax Town in 1911 when they were playing in the Yorkshire Combination. In his first season he played 29 games and scored 24 goals including four hat tricks. The following season the club joined the Midlands Counties League and for the next three seasons 'Judd', as he was known, continued his goal scoring with another eighteen in 54 games. There was no competition from 1916 to 1919, but in the first season after the war, 1920–21 he played in 23 games, scoring twelve times. A short-term transfer to Bradford City at the end of the season saw him return to the Shay, and in the football league he played 35 games scoring seventeen times. To recognise his service to the club he was granted a testimonial in 1924.

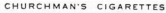

CHURCHMAN'S CIGARETTES

A card from Churchman's Association Footballers. The information on the reverse of the card gives the following information: 'Ernest Coleman who was born in Nottinghamshire first gained distinction as a centre forward but later developed into a clever constructive inside forward. Entering first class football with Halifax Town, he moved to Grimsby in 1929 and became notable for his scoring feats for the east Anglian club. In March 1932 he was transferred to the Arsenal at a fee of £8,000 and won a championship medal. Two years later he left to go to Middlesborough, and it was while he was with the Yorkshire club that he was converted into an inside forward. Since that time he was carried on successfully in this position with Norwich City, obtaining many goals.'

E. COLEMAN (NORWICH CITY)

The Picture House was one of the first purpose-built cinemas to be built in Halifax. It opened its doors on 20 October 1913 and closed in May 1982, taking the total number of cinema closures in the town to over 20. During its 69-year history it was renamed twice, firstly as the Gaumont and later the Astra. This photograph dates from around 1916.

Halifax Post Office is situated on Commercial Street. This building was designed by H. Tanner and was opened on 23 June 1887. It was the fifth post office in the town. The previous ones had been in Winding Road, which was opened in 1790, Cheapside, Westgate and George Street. The need for more space and facilities for the growing population called for a larger, purpose-built property in the heart of the town. The façade has little changed today, although the inside is vastly different to the 1887 version!

Joseph Crossley's Almshouses were made available to people over 60 who were incapacitated by work. However, they had to be of good character and had to have been involved in a Protestant Trinitarian church for a minimum of two years. They were designed by Roger Ives and were intended for ex-employees of John Crossley & Sons Ltd., carpet manufacturers. The first 21 homes were built in 1863 in the Gothic Revival style with turrets, oriels and a crenelated tower. The 21 homes formed three sides of a rectangle around a garden with a chapel on the south side. In 1868 a further 27 homes were planned, but Joseph Crossley's sudden death that year presented legal problems with the plans. However, an Act of Parliament in 1869 allowed his son Edward to carry out the plans. These have been modernised over the years and are still in use.

Old Market was an early site for the town's markets. The market cross was here, recorded in the 1790s as being three storeys high with an ugly cross and stone steps. Also standing here was the pillory, a device of punishment for lawbreakers of all kinds. The victims were secured in the pillory by neck and hands in a standing position, whilst passers by threw objects and abuse at them. Women were excused this embarrassment. It was removed in 1786 and abolished in 1837. In 1790 a new market was opened on Southgate, on the site of the present day Borough Market.

This bus was on its way to the village of Mount Tabor which can be seen at the top left of the photograph. There were plans to run a tram line from Pellon to Mount Tabor, but the gradient was so steep that the plans were rejected and a trolley bus service was introduced at the end of the First World War. Mount Tabor is north-west of Halifax near Pellon and is 1,038 feet above sea level at its highest point. The main industry in this area, particularly in the nineteenth century, was quarrying the local stone. This had been a trade in the Halifax area from the fourteenth century. The white building on the right side of the road is Broadley Laithe, a seventeenth century house and now a listed building.

Hansom cabs waiting for custom outside Halifax Station, designed by Manchester architect Thomas Butterworth. The Manchester to Leeds Railway was completed in 1841 but Halifax did not get its station until 1855, after developments in the cotton and wool trade created a need for faster transport. In the 1880s the station underwent major reconstruction to keep up with the growing population who used it and increasing freight traffic. In recent years, as in a lot of areas, the need for public rail transport has declined and the station is no longer at its best.

Until 1938 George Street was a narrow street of shops and offices with a single tram line, but that year the left side of the street was demolished for the widening of the road. There was talk of making it into a dual carriageway with gardens and the like, but there was concern as to how the people of Halifax would react to this major change, this being one of the first attempts at opening up streets. One of the buildings to be demolished was the offices of the *Halifax Guardian*. The paper had been published here from 1838 until it joined forces with the *Halifax Courier* in 1921. The building on the left with the arched windows is the Bull's Head, a large pub, and by the time of this photograph a Webster's House. Samuel Webster's Fountain Head Brewery was established in 1838 and supplied beer to all areas of Halifax and throughout Yorkshire and Lancashire. In the latter years of the twentieth century amalgamation with the brewing giants lead to the Fountain Head Brewery being closed. It was the last of three big Halifax breweries to follow the same route, the other two being Whitaker's and Ramsden's. The strange glass and white structure outside Liley's pram, toy and sewing machine shop was the upper entrance to underground public toilets.

This tram was travelling along the Huddersfield Road, now the A629. A couple of miles from the town centre is Salterhebble Hill, a steep section of road which caused some concern when the tramway was being planned. The gradient was reported to be 1 in 9.69 in a 1903 survey. This was thought to be a dangerous gradient and the hill also had bends. The Tram Committee considered installing a large lift to raise and lower the trams, and John Henry Whitley was sent to America to get opinions and advice from companies there using such devices. However, the lift was never installed. At the bottom of the hill is the Calder, which gets no nearer to the town than this, and also the Salterhebble Docks of the Calder & Hebble Navigation. John Henry Whitley (1866–1935) was born in Halifax and after gaining a BA at London University joined the family business of S. Whitley at Hanson Lane Mills. He became the Liberal MP for Halifax in 1900 and retained the seat until 1918. On 9 May 1919 he was made an Honorary Freeman of the borough. From 1921 to 1928 he was Speaker of the House of Commons. It was customary that retiring speakers received a knighthood but he was the first to decline the honour. In 1930 he became chairman of the BBC, and made the first broadcast on the Empire Service, which later was renamed the World Service. He is buried in Lister Lane Cemetery.

A view along Southgate, looking towards Halifax Town Hall. In the mid 1800s there were three sets of plans drawn up for a town hall, but nobody was impressed with any of them so the council invited Sir Charles Barry, architect of the Houses of Parliament, to do the job. Barry's price for the building was £22,000, higher than the council had budgeted for but they accepted the plans and work commenced in 1860. Tenders were accepted and it was evident that the original estimate was low. Whiteley Bros. of Leeds took on the job at £23,320 and in May of 1860 Sir Charles Barry died, when the

work had only just begun. His son Edward had been involved from the start and took over the project, the building being finished in 1863. The Prince of Wales opened the Town Hall on 4 August 1863 in front of a crowd of 60,000 people. The building was floodlit with approximately 16,000 batswing gas burners. The final bill was estimated at £50,126.

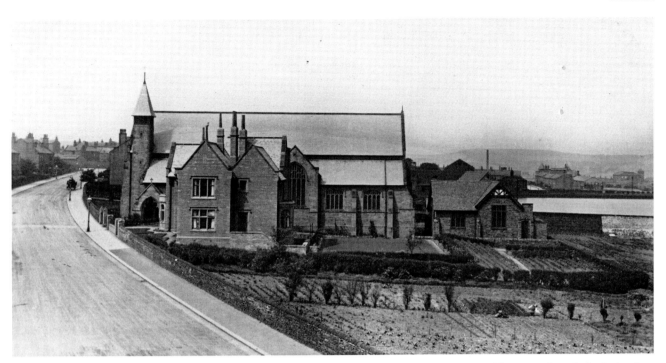

A section of Gibraltar Road overlooking the northern part of the town. The church is St Hilda's, seen here in isolation but today enclosed by close neighbours. The first sod cut for its construction was on 14 August 1909 and the building was finished and ready for consecration on 27 May 1914. The building was designed by Sutcliffe & Sutcliffe. Arthur Selby McCrea donated money to the building fund. He was part of the family business who owned H.C. McCrea, who dealt with stuff, damasks, reps and tapestries. In 1923 he bought Shibden Hall, part of the deal being that when he died the hall would be passed onto the council.

Halifax tram No. 87 making its way down Godley lane to Stump Cross on its way to Brighouse. This tram route was first used in 1904. Two women are looking towards the camera from the doorway of the H. Smith bakery and confectionery shop on the left of the picture. Next door is a parcel office. H. Fielden has a business next door but it is not clear what he was offering. On the other side of the road is the Museum Hotel selling Stock's ales. The single storey building on the corner is the old toll house.

St Jude's Church on Free School Lane, opposite Savile Park Moor. The building was designed by Halifax architect W. Swinden Barber in the late 1880s and was consecrated on 13 November 1890. A single clock was added in 1893, which had been obtained from Bowling Dyke Mills. In 1915 this was replaced with the four face one seen here. The original building had been designed and built at a cost of £8,400. Opposite the church is the drinking fountain that was donated by Joseph Thorpe, a local J.P., in 1869.

The Halifax Soldiers' Monument stands in West View Park, High Road Well, and overlooks Calderdale. The monument was unveiled on 7 November 1904 to honour the 73 Halifax soldiers who lost their lives in the South African or Boer Wars in the last years of the nineteenth century. West View Park was given to the town by two local mill owners, Henry Charles McCrae and Enoch Robinson, and opened in 1897 (McCrae was Halifax mayor in 1869–70, as was Robinson in 1904–05). The bronze soldier was blown off the monument in 1937 and replaced the following year. Also in 1937 the three field guns in the photo were removed as the timber was found to be rotten.

The Prince of Wales visited Halifax on 15 October 1926 to open Shibden Park. In this postcard he is seen planting a young oak tree that had been dug up from the heavily wooded slopes of the park. He was to become Edward VIII and is remembered for other things rather than his tree planting skills. On his short trip to Halifax he also toured Ladyship and Dean Clough mills.

Wainhouse Tower stands between Sowerby Bridge and King Cross and is in fact the chimney for the Washer Lane Dye Works. The mill is 200 yards away in the valley, but in order to disperse the smoke effectively the chimney was erected in a high position, the smoke rising through an underground flue to reach the chimney. John Edward Wainhouse, who owned the mill, decided that such a prominent chimney should be a feature of the area and he commissioned Isaac Booth to design it. Booth also worked for Sir Henry Edwards, who owned a neighbouring estate. Edwards and Wainhouse did not see eye to eye so Booth dropped out of the project. In 1874 Wainhouse sold the mill and the new owner was left with an unfinished chimney so he employed Richard Swarbrick Dugdale, who had been a pupil of Booth, to design the tower that can be seen today. It is an octagonal stone structure 253 feet high with an internal brick-built flue. In between the flue and the exterior are 403 steps that lead to the top balcony. From here rise sixteen 20-foot columns that support the upper balcony with lantern, dome and finial.

Saville Hall, Halifax. In the 1870s John Lewis was living at this property. He was a carpet manufacturer who had two mills in Halifax, India Buildings and Alhambra Works. In 1876 Halifax High School for girls leased this property from John Lewis for £150 per year. The school opened in January 1877 and accommodated 130 pupils including girls of secondary school age and boys up to the age of nine. As numbers increased the school had to use alternative premises for some of the classes, including the classroom at the Bluecoat School. A decision to move to larger premises was taken at the end of the 1920s, and Craven Lodge was purchased and demolished. On 21 June 1930 the foundation stone of the new Princess Mary's High School was laid by Mrs Howard Clay and it was officially opened on 21 September 1931 by the school's namesake.

Savile Road runs from Harrison Road to Savile Park Road and contains mostly detached properties, many of them listed and the majority named rather than numbered. One property Savile Lodge was in the 1800s owned by John Crossley JP, 1812–1879, third son of John Crossley, carpet manufacturer. In 1837 he became senior partner in John Crossley and Sons and from 1864 to 1877 was chairman. Kirkby Leas, another property, had been built in the early 1800s and in February 1933 was taken over by the Halifax King Edward VII Memorial District Nursing Association. They used the premises until 1970. The building was in the path of the proposed Burdock Way, the through town high level by-pass. It was left unoccupied, was vandalised and suffered from damp and rot and was demolished in 1970. In the 1911 census Thomas Fakes and family lived at No. 19. Thomas was born in Bury St Edmunds in 1860 and took a job as a domestic chauffeur in Halifax. The two roads either end of Savile road were very similar as far as properties were concerned. Harrison Road, originally called Harrison Lane, was lined by private houses and public buildings. Halifax Police Station was opened here on 29 October 1900 and contained the borough police and magistrates courts.

Princess Street and Southgate packed with thousands of people on 10 May 1910 to hear the Mayor, Alderman F. Whitley Thomson, read the proclamation of the accession to the throne of King George V. The mayor made the announcement from the balcony of the Town Hall.

Southgate, VE Day.

Halifax Rugby League Football Club was founded as a rugby union club in 1873. They were one of the 22 clubs who withdrew from the Rugby Union in 1895 to form the Northern Union. This was the result of a meeting held at the George Hotel in Huddersfield where several northern clubs wanted to reimburse some of their players for lost time from work. The Rugby Union were strictly amateur and would not sanction this, hence the breakaway. Rules were gradually changed over the following years and the two codes grew apart. The Northern Union became the Rugby League in 1922. Their home ground for 112 years was Thrum Hall about a mile from the town centre, the highest ground in the Rugby League. They were a successful team in the early days, winning the Championship in 1907, Division 1 in 1902, the Challenge Cup in 1903, 1904 and 1931 (and beaten finalists in 1921), the Yorkshire Cup in 1908 and the Yorkshire League in 1909 and 1921. This photograph shows the 1935–36 team.
Back row, left to right: F. Brindle, A. Childs, M. Meek, J. Treen, H. Irving, H. Jones, G. Baytham and J. Cox.
Front row, left to right: H. Lockwood (captain), F. Rule, R. Thomas, L. Sowden, D. Hickey.

An early team photograph of Halifax Northern Union Rugby club, taken sometime between 1906 and 1910.
Back row, left to right: I. Bartle, J. Swinbank, W.W. Williams, Mr Tyson (President), J.E. Jones, H. Wilson, G.H. Langhorne, J.W. Bulmer and Mr. Ricketts.
Seated row, left to right: F. Mallinson, A.J. Brown, R.S. Winskill, G. Kitson, J.A, Rigg, Joe Riley and J. Riley.
Front row, left to right: A. Nettleton, W.B, Little, H. Summerskill, H. Hadwen.
Langhorne, Rigg, Riley and Little are all in the Halifax Rugby League Hall of Fame.

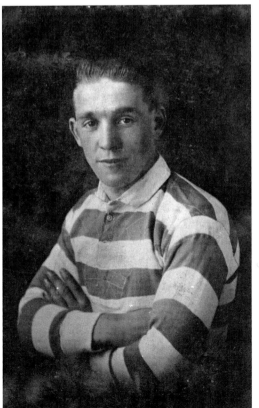

Top left: Arthur Peckett played for Halifax in the mid 1920s. The club have been at times amongst the best in the Rugby League as well as suffering periods in the doldrums. The 1950s and 60s were a good time, followed by a mediocre period until an influx of young Australians in the 1980s helped the club to Wembley victory and a Championship victory in consecutive seasons. In its days at Thrum Hall, before it moved to the Shay (which it shares with the football club), its ground could be an advantage in games against superior opposition. One corner of the ground dropped away quite steeply, and the home players had learned to use this to their advantage. On top of this Thrum Hall was the highest ground in the Rugby League, with at times, especially in the times of winter rugby, some severe weather. Thrum Hall was also the home of the cricket club and in the late 1890s there were three County Championship cricket matches here. Around the cricket pitch was the greyhound racing track and there was also an area for crown green bowls. All this is now no longer, the space having been taken by an Asda.

Top right: A member of the 1920–21 Halifax Rugby squad which won the Yorkshire League and also reached the Challenge Cup final. The players were promised bonuses for progress in the cup competition. A first round win would add £2 to their regular £4, second round £3, third round £4, £5 for semi-final victory and £10 each for winning the cup. Huddersfield were beaten in the semi final at Headingley, Leeds, in front of 23,500 spectators. The final was at The Cliff, the home of Broughton Rangers, a Manchester-based club where 25,000 turned up to watch the game. Halifax were favourites to pick up the trophy and their £6 bonus as they held a much higher league position. Leigh, however were the stronger team on the day, taking the cup 13–0. The Halifax players earned only their losing pay of £2.50 each.

Left: Charlie Rowlands was signed by Halifax Rugby League club for the beginning of the 1924–25 season. He was signed from Glynneath Rugby Union Club. Heavy unemployment in South Wales meant that more and more rugby union players were accepting rugby league offers which normally meant a job as well as a playing contract.

Sowerby Bridge

Sowerby Bridge is about three miles south-west of Halifax, at the confluence of the rivers Calder and Ryburn. The population at the 2011 census was 11,703. As its name suggests it was originally a crossing point of the River Calder, giving access for the townsfolk of Sowerby to the merchants of Halifax. The crossing place is County Bridge, a listed structure and the scene of a battle during the Civil War.

In recent years the town has been a market town, but from the early 1800s wool and cotton spinning were big business here. This was helped when the canals arrived, linking the town directly with Liverpool and the cotton imported from the Americas, and also giving the town a wider sales market.

When the canal was used for transporting goods, Sowerby Bridge was an important part of the system. The two canal systems that meet at the town had different sized locks making it impossible for the 70-foot boats from Lancashire to continue along the Calder and Hebble when their locks were only 57½ feet long. So boats had to be emptied and reloaded, providing plenty of work for locals, and warehouses had to be built for storage of goods. In recent times the Rochdale Canal has been reopened and the rebuilt Tuel Lane Lock has become the deepest lock in the United Kingdom, dropping the water level to allow passage under the road. This area has now been redeveloped, with a number of restaurants and bars utilising the buildings.

A view of Sowerby Bridge, with Norland in the right background. The tower belongs to Christ Church, the parish church, which opened on 24 May 1821. It replaced 'The Old Brigg Chapel', which had stood for almost 300 years on the banks of the Calder opposite its junction with the Ryburn. The industrial revolution had reached the area by the early 1800s and a larger church was required to accommodate the growing population. Land was purchased from Timothy Bates and James Goodhall on a site which is now along Wharf Street. The architect was John Oates and the new church cost in the region of £7,000 to complete. Over the years there have been several additions and alterations: the clock was added in 1839, the bells and organ in 1866, the church was extended and a chancel was added in 1873, and in 1889 a new vestry was built at the south door. In 1935 a chancel screen was donated to the church by Percy Carter. There is a war memorial inside the building, dated 1921, that records 64 names of men connected with the church who died in the First World War. There is also a communion table dated 1520 which was in the original church.

This is the gate house of Lower Willow Hall, Cote Hill, Halifax. The original hall and this gate house was built by Samuel King in 1635 and he lived here from 1640 to 1655. His surname was used to name the area of King Cross between Sowerby Bridge and Halifax. The family moved to Mytholm Hall in Hebden Bridge in 1655 and King died in 1674. The Ciff, Barstow and Lower Bairstow had all been previous names of Lower Willow Hall. Other occupants over the years have included Abraham Frank who was in occupation in 1710, Edmund Lodge in 1774, John Swallow in 1861 and William Wood in 1904. In 1783 the Lees family were living at the Hall and operating the Lower Willow Hall Mills, which may have been the first cotton spinning mill in the area. The Hall was demolished and rebuilt in 1792, and extended in 1860, but the gate house is all that remains of the site. It is now a private house and a listed building.

Walter Lees was born in Sowerby Bridge on Christmas Day, 1875. He played first class cricket for Surrey and London County and represented England five times on their 1906 tour of South Africa. He was an all rounder, scoring 7,642 runs, with a top score of 137 and taking 1,402 wickets with a best innings figure of 9 for 81. His international career went no further than his 5 test matches in South Africa where he scored 66 runs and took 26 wickets. He died on the 10th September 1924 in West Hartlepool.

Crow Wood is situated at the top of Bolton Brow, between Sowerby Bridge and King Cross. The surrounding grounds are now Crow Wood Park, the entrance to which is the Sowerby Bridge war memorial. On 25 April 1917 the house became Crow Wood V.A.D. Hospital. V.A.D. stands for Voluntary Aid Detachment and the house was a hospital and recuperation unit for up to 50 wounded or otherwise damaged men shipped back from France. Day duties were carried out by the Voluntary Aid Detachment and the night shift was covered by the 8th Battalion Women's Royal Volunteer section. In charge of the hospital was Commandant Matron Gowing, which makes it sound more like a prison camp!

This is probably a gathering of Sunday school pupils outside St Paul's Methodist Chapel on Tuel Lane. This site has been occupied by several buildings over the years, the first going back to 1851. Five local preachers had been expelled from the Wesleyan church and were conducting services and other meetings in either private houses or at the Bull's Head. In 1850 they raised enough money to buy this plot of land and build the first chapel. It was a single-storey building with a Sunday school underneath and was called the Tuel Lane United Methodist's Free Chapel, also known as the Reformer's Chapel. It was opened around 1853 and was demolished twenty years later. A larger building replaced it at a cost of £2,800, but within five years the people of the chapel became unhappy with the way it had been built so the inside was removed and rearranged with a new organ at a cost of £2,300. Rebuilding the gables and sorting out the gas lighting cost another £850. In 1897 a house was acquired for the preacher at a cost of £500. By 1900 the chapel seen here had been built and it was modernised in 1979. On Easter Day 1988 the chapel was damaged by a suspected arson attack and a new chapel was opened on the site in 1990.

This photograph of Wharf Street was probably taken from the top deck of a tram. To the left of the photographer is the junction with Tuel Lane and the view is looking towards Halifax. The single-track tram line ran down the centre of the road allowing other vehicles to pass either side, although that meant people wanting to use the tram had to cross the roadway to get on or off. This tram line ran between Halifax and Triangle and to keep the service as regular as needed there had to be passing points where a second run of track was laid parallel to the main line to allow trams to pass each other. There were two such places in the town, one by the County Bridge (behind the photographer here) and the other a couple of hundred yards further along Wharf Street.

The gradient of Lower Clifton Street is 1 in 3.7 and it picked up a couple of local nicknames, T'Delph and Spion Kop, the latter being one that stuck, named after the famous battle of the South African War. The mill chimney showing between the houses was part of Brearley's Mill; the chimney has gone and after a fire so has the mill. Some demolition has been done in recent times along the street and concrete obstructions have been placed across the road to prevent people from driving up it. The photo was taken from Bolton Brow.

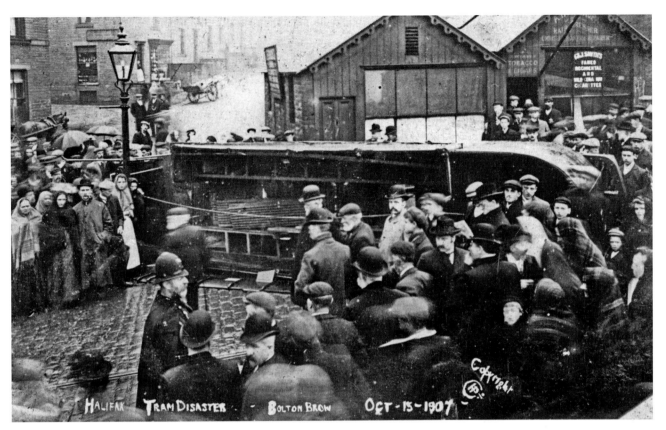

On Tuesday, 15 October 1907 the No. 64 tram from Triangle to Halifax passed through Sowerby Bridge, making its way up to Bolton Brow to follow Pye Nest Road into King Cross and on into Halifax. This section of road out of Sowerby Bridge, which is 1 in 13, was damp and slippery and the early morning tram was packed with people on their way to work, making this a difficult climb. As the tram reached Pye Nest, opposite Edwards Road, there was a power failure affecting the King Cross to Sowerby Bridge section and it came to a standstill, and then started to roll backwards down Bolton Brow. A passenger tried to apply the brake as did the conductor, but the momentum of the vehicle combined with the wet rails was too much. The tram gathered speed, lost its power pick up and as the two tracks up Pye Nest converged into a single track, the tram left the rails, fell onto its side, spun round, mounted the pavement and crashed into a shop front, demolishing the shop. The top deck had broken away from the tram and the whole wreckage ended up outside the school, but thankfully this was at 5.45 a.m. before any children had arrived for classes. Nonetheless, five of the 70 passengers died and 42 were injured. Subsequently, the transport management in Halifax brought in new safeguards to try to prevent similar accidents from happening. There is a memorial to the conductor at Mount Chapel, Ogden.

This is the bar house or toll house that stood at the junction of West Street and Watson Mill Lane. At the bottom of the lane was a bridge crossing the Ryburn, allowing access to Norland. This had to be paid for as the roads were maintained by the local population and funds had to be available for repairs. Originally there were gates across the road, but these were removed in 1872. The house remained until demolition in the 1980s. There is a story about an unnamed man who drank at the West Bottom Tavern in Norland: he claimed that he could push a wheelbarrow from Watson Mill Lane to Triangle faster than the tram and he succeeded by pushing the barrow along the tram lines in order to block the tram from passing him. A few years after the opening of the Rishworth branch railway line, Watson Crossing Halt was made at the bottom of Watson Mill Lane. By the second half of the 1920s this branch line was in decline due to the tram service and the subsequent buses, and the two tracks had been cut to one, the second being used as a storage facility. There was an accident on the line in 1926 when a train of empty coaches stored on the line began to move towards Sowerby Bridge and derailed at Watson Crossing. 112 coaches were involved in the incident but there were no injuries.

This card was produced to celebrate the retirement of the Rev. George Samuel Smith in 1905. The photographs on the card feature the vicar in the centre and young men from the Sunday school. The Rev. Smith was born in Lowestoft and had been vicar at Harrison Road Chapel in Halifax. He moved to Gosport but in 1881 he moved back to take over at Sowerby Bridge. The West End Congregational Church was built on land bought from William Eddleston, a local mill owner, and it opened in 1880. In 1909 there was a donation from Andrew Carnegie towards a new organ. The building was also used by the Sowerby Bridge YMCA and the local Golden Age Club. In 1897 a Sunday school was built next to the church. This was a large building with 11 classrooms, a balcony and a minister's vestry. In 1957 the church was closed and in time was demolished to make way for petrol station.

This straight stretch of road at Belmont links Sowerby Bridge and Triangle. The tram is coming from Triangle with its destination advertised as Post Office: this would be Halifax Post Office on Commercial Street, a regular drop-off point for trams and buses for many years. To the right of the tram can be seen an older form of transport! To the left is Belmont Terrace which no longer stands.

A view down Bolton Brow from its junction with Wakefield Road. The tower left of centre belongs to Christ Church Parish Church, and behind it can be seen Sowerby church. A couple of shops can be seen in Bolton Brow, but the main shopping street in Sowerby Bridge is Wharf Street, which can be seen at the foot of the hill.

1887. A SOUVENIR. 1917.

Rev. C. Ll. IVENS, M.A.,
Vicar.

Rev. CANON IVENS, M.A.,
Vicar.

Christ Church, Sowerby Bridge.

This card shows Canon Charles Llewelyn Ivens at both ends of his 30-year ministry at Christ Church, Sowerby Bridge. He became famous, not just locally but over a wide area, for his 'men's services' which attracted congregations that filled the church. After one such service on 4 February 1894 disaster struck the church as a fire broke out in the organ and quickly spread to the roof. The fire brigades from both Halifax and Sowerby Bridge fought the blaze and although the roof was badly damaged, it did not fall. Sadly Jonathan Coulston, a fire-fighter, fell through a trapdoor in the tower and died on the steps below. Repair work and a few alterations saw the church out of commission for twelve months. It was reopened on 2 February 1895.

A general view of the west end of Sowerby Bridge. The railway bridge can just be made out to the lower right and the tower of the Town Hall is in the centre. In front of the large mill in the bottom left is the Ryburn which joins with the Calder as it passes under the railway bridge. All the terraced housing on the hill side can be accessed from Tuel Lane. These would have been mill workers cottages in the late 1800s and early 1900s. The market place was at river level in the bottom right, hidden behind the cottage. Much of the industry has vanished from the town and the market has also been reduced and relocated to a much smaller undercover new build site along Wharf Street.

The Triangle to Halifax tram just starting the climb up Bolton Brow. The journey to this point was more or less on the flat, but not much further up the slope increases to 1 in 13, before levelling off again for the gradual gentle slope into Halifax. Within 100 yards up the hill from the position of this tram was the resting place of the tram that derailed in 1907, killing four passengers, the conductor and injuring many others. The steepness of the hill is still a hazard today.

Ten to eleven in the morning, looking down Wharf Street on what appears to be a summer's day. In the left bottom corner of the photograph is the end of Tuel Lane. On the corner is a clothes shop with what appears to be a pattern book on a stand by the door, so it was probably a tailor as well. The next two shops are essential in any town, a baker's and a butcher's, with the butcher standing on the kerb looking towards the camera.

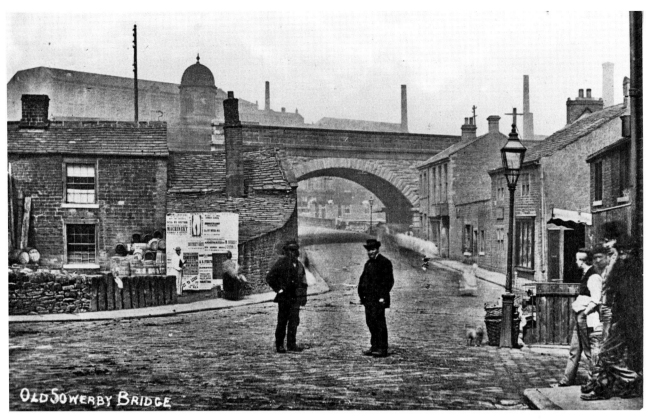

This postcard was posted in 1910, but the photograph itself is much older. The two men are standing in the road that leads to Sowerby; beyond the railway bridge it leads into the town. Just to the left of the bridge and the chimney is the dome of the Town Hall. The clock was installed in 1863. The cottages to the right behind the gas lamp and butting up to the bridge were replaced with the Ryburn Buildings and the entrance to Station Road in 1884 so the photograph was taken sometime before that year.

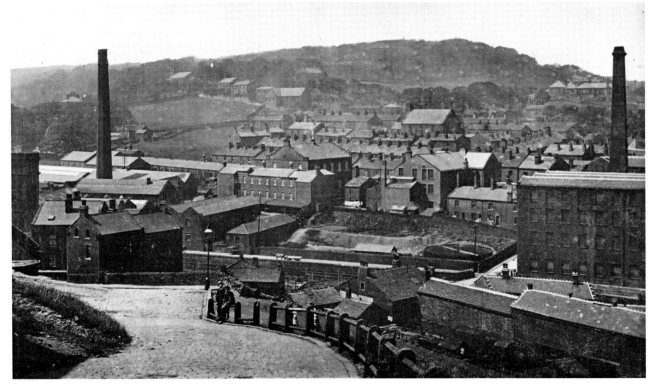

The west end of town, viewed from the Norland side of the valley. The opposite hill is part of Sowerby village. Just to the left of the mill on the right side of the photo is an open sewage treatment plant.

Some members of the Sowerby Bridge Grammar School rugby team photographed outside the cricket pavilion on Albert Road. The school was basically a football and cricket school with rugby being a third option.
Back row, left to right: Ian Ford, Alistair McDonald, Peter Rushby, Philip Sunderland, Roger Bottonley.
Front row, left to right: Richard Smith, Robert Walker, Kevin Hallowell, Guy Standeven, ? Gibson.

Watson Mills, Sowerby Bridge. This mill, in the Ryburn Valley on the way to Triangle, covered almost five acres and was both a corn and cotton mill in its time. Just behind the smoking chimney in the centre of the photograph is the Sowerby Bridge to Rishworth branch line and there was a halt here called Watson Crossing. The mill was closed in the 1960s and finally demolished in 1978 after a fire. The road crossing the railway line is leading up to Norland.

Triangle

The village of Triangle stands either side of the A58 between Sowerby Bridge and Ripponden. The original road through Triangle passed through Mill Bank on its way to Lancashire, but the new turnpike road took a different route and branched off left to continue on to Ripponden. This left a triangular piece of land at the junction, hence the name of the village although it was originally known as Stansfield's Pond or just Pond. The Triangle Inn was built on this section of land in the mid 1760s, and from 1777 the village was called Triangle. The village has Sowerby on one hillside and Norland on the other. Mills were the main source of employment in the village with several nearby and one of its own, Stansfield Mill. From the 1880s to the 1920s Triangle had its own station on the Rishworth Branch, albeit quite a distance from the village, and it was also the end of the line for the tram service from Halifax along the Ryburn Valley. Triangle Cricket Club has been in the village for 150 years, playing their first games in 1862. The ground, Grassy Bottom, is beside the Ryburn and at the back of Stansfield Mill, the latter now much smaller after some demolition due to unstable stonework (the secure part of the mill has since been transformed into modern apartments). The ground was gifted to the club by mill owner Col. T. H. Morris in 1927. Originally the club was associated with the local reading room and called Triangle Reading Room Cricket Club and nobody could play cricket without being a member of the reading room. The reading room stressed abstention from intoxicating beverages and encouraged exercise in open air. By the 1960s however the club was one of only two or three in the Halifax Cricket League to run a bar in the pavilion!

The Stile Triangle was the terminus of the Halifax tram, leaving the residents of Ripponden, Rishworth and surrounding areas reliant on the train, walking or horse transport. All the trams on this single-track route were open topped so that they could get under the railway bridge at Sowerby Bridge, where there was also a passing place. On the left of the photo, about level with the tram, are three rows of terraced houses: East Street, Middle Street and West Street. These were built up at right angles to the road and extended up the hill from the footpath. In recent years these terraces have been shortened and new properties take up the land by the road. Between the two tram poles were a few small shops, no longer there. Over the years these were a bakery, fish and chip shop, plumber's shop, hardware shop, decorator's store and probably more. The white building on the right of the photograph is still there, but is now a house. The view looks towards Sowerby Bridge.

STANSFIELD MILL

Stansfield Mill was built in the early nineteenth century. The Stansfield family were major local landowners and lived at Field House, a large Georgian house on Dean Lane overlooking Triangle. Behind the house was a walled garden that produced enough fruit and vegetables to feed a small village, and beside the house was a boating lake with boathouse and two tennis courts, along with extensive gardens. In 1848 the mill was taken over by William Morris and Sons, worsted spinners. In 1875 they expanded when they built the Corporation Mill beside the canal in Sowerby Bridge to become one of the largest spinning companies in the West Riding of Yorkshire, with around 600 workers recorded in 1890. In the late 1970s the mill at Triangle was found to be structurally unsound and all work was moved to the Sowerby Bridge Mill. In 1985 part of the Stansfield Mill was demolished but some of it was transformed into apartments. The Morris Family were generous to the local community who provided the majority of their workforce. In 1862 they gave a plot of land overlooked by the mill to Triangle Cricket Club. Near the river, a long handled net is always on hand for the rescue of cricket balls! Field House has been converted into apartments.

The top left image on this postcard shows Alexandra Bridge which is at Kebroyd, on the Ripponden side of Triangle. This bridge replaced a set of stepping stones sometime prior to 1913. The path leads to Norland and there are several cottages in the wood that could also be reached this way. Also in the wood there was a tea room called Littlehaven, which is now a private house. Bottom right is described elsewhere. The other two are general shots of the village. Bottom left shows Thorpe House and mill which belonged to a Mr Rawson. This photograph was taken from the hillside above the Rishworth Branch. The centre image was also taken from the hillside, this time on route to Mill Bank.

Mill House Lodge, on the road between Triangle and Sowerby Bridge. The gates in the foreground led to Mill House, a Victorian residence built for the Rawson family who were mill owners in the Ryburn Valley. The house has been demolished but the lodge survives. The open-topped trams from Sowerby Bridge started to pass the lodge on 7 February 1905, and the last one passed on 25 July 1934, when the service was terminated.

A shot of St John the Divine Church and Sunday school, Triangle, taken from somewhere near the Rishworth Branch. The hills in the background are part of the village of Millbank. This is a very old established village, built around the cloth trade, with records of a fulling mill here in the fourteenth century. Most of the buildings date back to the seventeenth century. The village is on the old trade route between Yorkshire and Lancashire. In the nineteenth century there were five woollen and silk mills in the village. Kebroyd mills were close by and provided work for some villagers, but fires there in 1901 and 1904 meant closures until they were rebuilt. In 1970 the Sowerby Bridge Urban District Council came up with plans to demolish the whole village but these were dropped due to considerable opposition. The church was built for F. E. Rawnson who lived at nearby Thorpe House. It was one of the first churches in the country to be built from reinforced concrete, cost £7,000 to build and was consecrated on 23 September 1880. In 1914 the church was amalgamated with Saint Mary's Church at Cottonstones and in 1917 the building was badly damaged by fire, repairs taking six years. On its demolition the font was moved to Saint George's Church, Sowerby. The last service held there was on 9 June 1968 and five years later it was demolished. The two-storey Sunday school was built in 1882.

The Lodge is situated at the top of Stansfield Mill Lane and was the home of the Morris family. The photograph shows the house in 1920, still the family residence at that point, but in the following year it was converted into a hostel. There was not a sufficient workforce in the village to run all the local mills, so the Morris family came up with a plan to bring in girls from other areas of the country such as Doncaster and Durham. The Lodge was capable of housing around 100 girls who were looked after by a matron and other staff. Many of the girls married local lads and settled in the area. In 1970 the mill became unstable and work was transferred to the family's other mill in Sowerby Bridge, so there was no longer a need for the Lodge. It was converted into apartments and renamed Stansfield Grange.

Ripponden

Ripponden stands at the junction of three roads, the Oldham Road which passes through Rishworth on its way to Lancashire, the Rochdale Road and the Elland Road, which leads to the nearby villages of Barkisland, Stainland, Norland and Greetland. The 2011 census gives a population of 4,665.

The surrounding hills are of archaeological interest, not just for the Roman road that passes over Blackstone Edge, but for Neolithic and Bronze Age remains. Ripponden was a mill town in the nineteenth century and in the first half of the twentieth, but now most of the mills are gone whilst others have been converted into apartments or work and storage units. At one point there was a plan to cut a canal from Sowerby Bridge to the village to make transportation of raw materials and finished goods easier but instead the railway arrived in 1878. A branch line two miles and 76 chains (a cricket pitch length of 22 yards) long was constructed from Sowerby Bridge. The land had been surveyed 33 years earlier but there were many objections from local landowners.

The branch was extended to Rishworth in 1881. At that time, according to a report produced in the 1880s, the five miles of the Ryburn Valley contained 38 mills which produced 6,800 tons of raw materials per year and 9,000 tons of finished goods. All this was previously transported to and from Sowerby Bridge Station by horse and cart! However, the line was reasonably short lived. The passenger service ended in 1929 and the goods in 1958.

Ripponden was a forerunner in its foundation of a Cooperative Society which first opened its doors on 1 December 1832. The first shop was at Pleasant Row in the village and in the 1840s a branch was opened at Triangle, followed in 1847 by one at Bolton Brow, Sowerby Bridge. In Ripponden there was a general store, drapery, boot and shoe shop, and a butchery department with its own slaughterhouse and piggery. All this gradually faded away with increased public transport and the introduction of supermarkets.

RPN. 101.   RYBURN DAM. RIPPONDEN.

Ryburn Dam is known locally as Bogden because the Bogden was a tributary of the Ryburn, and a local beauty spot, which joined with the Ryburn at this point before the dam was built. Work on the dam began on 15 July 1925, when the first sod was cut, and took eight years to complete, finally opening on 7 September 1933. The dam covers an area of 26 acres and holds 220 million gallons of water, and the dam wall is more than 100 feet high. The total cost for the construction of the dam was £240,000. Wakefield Corporation planted 60,000 spruce and larch trees around the dam which have matured over the years, making this a very pleasant area to visit. Paths around the dam allow access to Parrock Nook and Rochdale Road. This was the first of three dams built on the Ryburn to supply water to Wakefield.

Just a few of the 200 or so men employed to build the Ryburn Dam. It is thought that the older man on the left may have been the explosives expert; if so his stone-built hut can still be seen when the waters of the Ryburn Reservoir are low. Many of these workers were not local men as a small shanty village of huts was erected to house them. Stansfield Hey, a nearby house, was taken over as a boardroom and lodging for the chief engineer. The stone required for the concrete was from nearby Hanging Lee Quarry and was taken to the on-site concrete mixers via a specially constructed two-foot-gauge railway.

Baitings Reservoir, Ripponden

Baitings Reservoir is situated above the Ryburn Dam, within a couple of miles of the watershed. The Ryburn Dam is clearly visible from here. The river is no more than a stream at this point, but still manages to fill both reservoirs most of the time. Work started here in 1948 to supply water to the city of Wakefield and took six years to complete. The dam is 200 feet high and contains 375,000 tons of concrete. The reservoir covers 64 acres and holds 775 million gallons of water. At the narrow end on the dam there is a bridge that takes the road over the water and this is a very scenic route to Parrock Nook and Rishworth. In the 1960s there was a track on the dry side of the wall that was used for vehicle hill races. The building at the side of the water is the New Inn, which is now a private residence, and the photographer is standing somewhere near the Blue Ball Inn, which is also now a dwelling.

Ryburn Dam as seen from Barr Lane. The three gaps in the top of the wall are the overflow system. For times of heavy rain and heavy overflow the banks of the river have been reinforced to protect the foundations of the road and properties near it.

A montage of the dam and its reservoir.

Five views of Bogden, prior to the building of the Ryburn Dam.

This postcard was produced to celebrate 60 years of the new Ripponden Church, 1868 to 1928. It shows the five vicars who had served there during that period. The Rev. James Sanders had been vicar in the old church and continued in the new building.

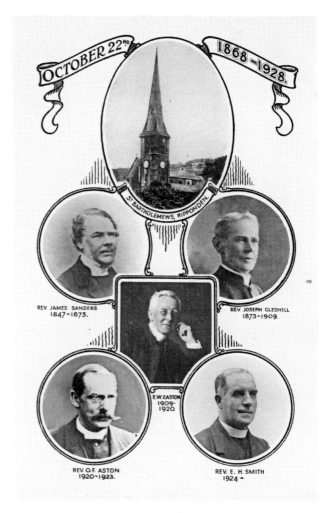

A view of the Ryburn Valley. The building with the gable showing to the front next to the terrace of houses is Stones Chapel and to the left of that is Stones School. These face onto the Rochdale Road less than a mile from Ripponden village. The three white buildings above the chapel are Rishworth School and they face onto the Oldham Road. These two roads meet at Ripponden to continue onto Halifax and beyond. The two roads follow the same route as the rivers, the Ryburn takes the Rochdale Road route, and the Booth Dene Clough the Oldham route. These converge less than a half mile from this scene. Rishworth, despite not being in the Ryburn Valley, has always been regarded as part of Ryburndale, with the Booth Dene Clough being a major tributary of the Ryburn.

Ripponden war memorial is situated in a small triangular garden at the junction of the Oldham and Rochdale roads. It lists 62 local men who did not return from the First World War and a further eighteen from the Second.

Ripponden and Barkisland Station. The branch line from Sowerby Bridge reached Ripponden in 1878, but it took another two years to extend the track to Rishworth. There were two plans for a line from Halifax to Lancashire, this branch line being the one that was rejected. The original plan was to continue the line up the Ryburn Valley, tunnel under the hills and come out near Littleborough, thence to Rochdale and on to Manchester. The second plan, decided the best, took the line up the Calder Valley instead, again linking up with Littleborough. The station buildings at Ripponden and Rishworth were identical, although the warehouse at the latter was larger. Two thousand people used the line on the opening day. Ripponden Brass Band played at the station and there were church bells and cannon fire to welcome the first train from Sowerby Bridge. There were first, second and third class coaches at 7d, 5d and 3½d. Traffic on the branch line decreased when the plans for the Calder Valley route became favoured, and the line started to operate on one track, with the other used for storage of excursion stock, etc. Passenger services were withdrawn in 1929 and goods in 1953. The branch line was finally abandoned in 1958. Ripponden's station was demolished and built on while Rishworth Station was left intact for about 20 years before meeting the same fate. The trackbed became an official nature trail.

This man, who may have been a postal or railway worker, is standing in a lane opposite the Zion Congregational Chapel on Oldham Road, Ripponden. The Zion Chapel has gone the way of a lot of properties in the area and is now private housing. It used to house the clinic in the 1950s where, one day a week, mothers with young children would go for their free bottle of orange juice.

A view of the River Ryburn between Slitheroe and Ripponden. There are some houses by the river and a path that leads from Ripponden to Rishworth. From Ripponden the path can be found in between the Packhorse Bridge and the church by going under the road bridge. The remains of Ripponden Mill are on the right but once past these the path is next to the river. After a quarter of a mile or so there is a footbridge that leads up to the main road beside the Besom pub. Ignoring the footbridge the path continues but not in such good order to Slitheroe, where again there is access to the main road. After that the path continues but gradually wanders away from the river, although it still leads in the same direction until it reaches Rishworth Mill. Mill Lane then leads up the main road.

The Packhorse Bridge crosses the Ryburn between the Old Bridge Inn and the church. There is mention of a bridge in the Wakefield Court rolls of 1316 but no description or information on its construction. In the early 1500s William Firth bequeathed seven shillings and seven pence for the making of a stone bridge over the Ryburn. In 1628 John Firth bequeathed 40 shillings for its repair. 1973 saw another repair, creating a very sharp apex not suitable for all vehicles. Originally there were no railings to the bridge, making it easier for packed animals or carts to cross as their loads were able to go beyond the wall without interference, but they appeared some time in 1800s after a man fell over the side and died in the river. On the Inn side of the bridge were the village stocks.

The Old Bridge Inn on Priest Lane is one of the oldest public houses in Yorkshire. It first gets a mention in records of 1307. Around 1815 the pub changed its name to the Waterloo after the battle, but soon officially reverted back to the original although the Waterloo name stuck with some families as late as the 1970s and 80s, both names being in local use. The inside of the pub has probably not much changed since Daniel Defoe stayed there on his journey across England in the 1700s. It has recently become the home of the Pork Pie Appreciation Society.

A general view of Ripponden. The earliest marked stone in the graveyard dates from 1657, but there were many buried here before this date who have no memorial. A small stream, Cob Clough, flows under the graveyard and into the Ryburn. In the days of the second Ripponden Church, Cob Clough flowed under the building as well as under the graves. However, on 18 May 1722 torrential rainfall raised the water level of the Ryburn by six feet. The Cob Clough also swelled and destroyed the church and several graves, washing them down river. One coffin lodged in a tree.

'James Booth, Ripponden' is written in pencil on the reverse of this photograph from the First World War. There are no Booths named on the Ripponden war memorial so this local man seems to have survived the conflict.

Ryburndale Paper Mill stood on Barr Lane off Slitheroe Bridge. Clean water is a priority for papermaking, so this mill was ideally placed getting first use of the Ryburn as it flowed down from Blackstone Edge. The Ryburn Dam was built about 300 yards upstream from the mill with a feeder pipe keeping the supply of clean water to the mill. The yard at the front of the mill was built over the river with storage sheds on the opposite bank. The mill specialised in paper for bibles, prayer books and other publications that required a high quality thin paper. The mill no longer stands and the site has been taken over by private housing. However, a path through the buildings can still be used to access the steps up either side of the dam.

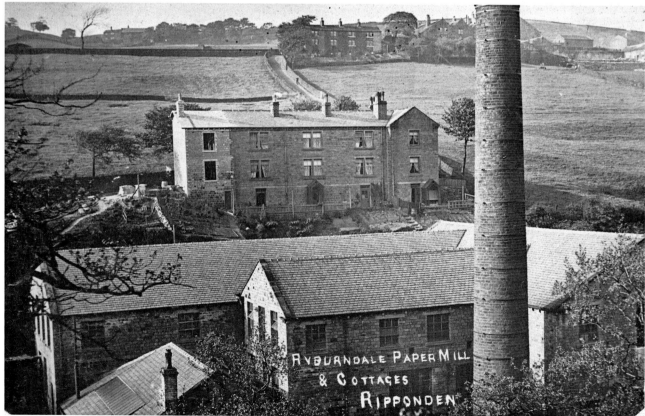

Saint Bartholomew's Church stands beside the old packhorse route, which today leaves the main road through the village as Priest Lane, crosses the old Packhorse Bridge, and by the church changes into Ripponden Old Bank. This is the fourth church to occupy this site, the earliest being built in the fifteenth century. Before that, with no place to worship in the village, people were forced to travel as far away as Elland for their Sunday service and they petitioned the Duke of York for a church of their own. It was finally King Edward IV who granted permission to cut timber and quarry stone for the building. In 1610 this building was replaced and was probably nearer to the river than the present one, because it was washed away by the Ryburn in flood. This resulted in a stone structure being built as the third church. This was demolished and the current church was built in 1868. Some of the internal pillars from the third church have been reused and some of the glass in the windows is thought to have been from the original church. This would have had an earth floor which once a year was covered with rushes to soak up moisture and help make the place cleaner and perhaps a little warmer. To celebrate the heritage of the village in recent years the Ripponden Rushbearing Ceremony has been reinstated, where in September hundreds of people go to the village to welcome the rush cart which, over two days of events, travels from Sowerby Bridge.

Ripponden, looking towards Sowerby Bridge. The white timbered building on the left is the Queen Hotel, built around 1800 as a coaching inn going by the name of the Stansfield Arms. Over the years the inn has also been known as the Prince of Orange, the Prince William and the Holroyd Arms. Next to the inn was a small waiting room where passengers would wait for the Liverpool to Halifax stagecoach. The bell to signal the arrival of the stage was at one time in the inn. The Queen has always been a meeting place for various groups and societies, including the Ripponden Female Society, founded in 1802 and the first society of its kind in the country. It provided sickness benefit to members and helped with funeral expenses and the like. In 1832 the Radical Party met here, whilst their opponents – the Tory Party – met next door in the Golden Lion. In the 1840s the innkeeper's daughter, Miss Bradley, became the first village post-mistress, the office being in the small building next to the hotel.

Holly Crescent is a small group of semi-detached houses built on a curve with a private access road and open grassed land to the front. They are built close to Slitheroe Bridge and back on to the premises of what was Ripponden and District Motors. Across the road is the Besom pub. Since this photograph was taken the grassed area to the front has been built on.

The toll-bar house for the road between Ripponden and Elland was originally on the corner between the cart and the people. When the tolls were ended in 1873 the building was demolished and rebuilt on top of the new shops that had recently been built. The shop underneath had so much glass that the corner was christened 'The Crystal Palace'. The toll was there to pay for the maintenance of the road and fees varied, depending on the customers: livestock, stagecoaches, wagons, horseback riders, etc., all paid different fees to use the road. A chain was stretched across the junction and not removed until the fee had been paid. There was an enforced road statute duty at this time which stated that anybody could be called upon to work repairing the roads. Mostly this was done by workhouse people but others could also be conscripted to work for beer and food only, breaking stones to fill pot holes and make the road safer. The Oldham to Ripponden Turnpike was opened in 1803. This was called the Cotton Route and brought an increasing amount of traffic and work into the village. So much so that the idea of a canal tunnel under the hills to Ripponden was seriously considered.

A photo of Ripponden Church taken from across the river, probably on the path that leads down the side of the Old Bridge Inn.

A view of Ripponden, looking towards Rishworth. The cobbled road to the left is Elland Road, the one to the right is for Rochdale and straight on for Rishworth. The white building on the right is the Golden Lion. The first mention of this as an inn dates from 1754 when it was called the Spout. This is probably named after the farm that occupied this site, first mentioned in 1673, and gets its name from a spring that surfaces at the rear of the property. The inn was a coaching stop and beside it were stables, long gone and now replaced by brick-built shops. The Golden Lion was also a post house. Letters would be left there and picked up by post riders who took them to Halifax, under armed guard fearing highway robbers. The post for the village and surrounding areas was then delivered from the inn. The innkeeper Thomas Hoyle would charge for delivery and would not allow people to pick up their own mail from the inn without paying the charge. Complaints to the Postmaster General eventually led to the official post office being opened at the Queen Hotel next door. The inn was renowned for its punch bowl and attracted the professional people from the village. Over the stables there was a reading room where the older men in the area could read the newspapers. In the 1800s a cattle market was held once a year on the forecourt .

An early photograph of the village centre. A cart is leaving on the road to Triangle. The white building on the left hand side of the road is the stable of the Golden Lion.

A view from the small triangular park at the junction of the Oldham and Rochdale roads. This is built around the war memorial that can be seen on the left. The building to the right was the post office and next to that is the Ryburn Rooms, where the council offices used to be. Behind the van was Terry's fish and chip shop and the pub is the Junction.

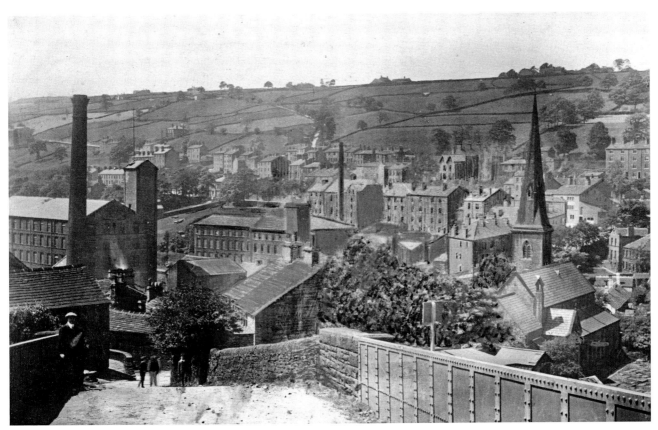

A view of Ripponden taken from the railway bridge on the Old Bank. The steepness of the roads and pathways is typical of the valley. The mill to the left is Chapel Field Mill. The tower with the gable was a lift. Most of this building has now gone, but some of the lower stories are still used for business. The second mill, just left of centre, is Ripponden Mill, known locally as 'Th' owd Bass'; this is also mostly gone, the remains being used for the same purpose as Chapel Field. Ripponden Mill was destroyed by fire three times and rebuilt twice. The first time was in 1858, then 1876 and finally in 1980. The tall houses between the centre mill chimney and the church are underdwellings. On the roadside these properties are normal two story houses, but because of the steep drop of the land to the river there could be two or three more stories at the back.

Ryburn House, situated on the main road between Ripponden and Triangle. This was originally a small cotton spinning mill built around 1790, with a house on the site for the mill owners. In 1861 the mill was owned by the Ripponden and District Spinning Co. Ltd, who rebuilt it. Within a year they went into liquidation due to the Cotton Famine, also known as the Cotton Panic. This was created by the shortage of cotton leaving the United States because of its civil war. Cotton mills in Lancashire and West Yorkshire bought 70% of their raw material from America and as a result a lot of mills closed and many people became unemployed. A larger mill was built nearby and this original one became a private house. One occupant was Dr Harold Murtagh, who was recorded as living there in 1937. He was a doctor from the old school: if called out away from the village he would always call in on other patients in the area to ask of their health and drink their tea.

This grocer's and confectioner's shop and house was just on the Ripponden side of Denton Bridge at Kebroyd. Whiteley Gee was manager of the Rishworth branch of the Ripponden Cooperative Society before taking on this shop. The business was taken over by Arthur Bennett, who is photographed elsewhere in this book as a member of Rishworth Baptist Concert Parties. The shop has since been converted into a private dwelling.

A nice view of the Old Bridge Inn and the church. The cobbled Priest Lane leads away to the right over the packhorse bridge and the scene looks almost the same today.

Unity Terrace is a short walk away from the village centre. The white building in the distance is the White Swan, which was known locally as the Mucky Duck. This is now a restaurant.

The ornate building on the right side of the road is the Ryburn Rooms. As well as being used for social events this was the home of Ripponden Council. A small office towards the near end of the building was where all locals had to go once a year to pay their rates. Long before direct debits, people queued to pay cash at a desk and pick up a handwritten receipt. The hills in the distance are on Norland Moor. There is no real centre to Norland, just a few farms, some cottages and the odd pub.

Wedding celebrations outside the Conservative Club. The bride and groom in the foreground are Mr and Mrs Michael Wheelwright and to their left are Mr and Mrs Wheelwright senior. The man with the banded trilby to the right of the groom is Herbert Staves and next to him is Mr Winders with his wife and daughter. The lady with white on a dark hat is Edith Eastwood. The guests were more than likely tenants or workforce of the Wheelwright family, who owned the majority of Rishworth.

Brig Royd House was the home of Mr and Mrs Ayres. He was a lawyer who worked in Manchester. The house was large and the grounds stretched down the side of Royd Lane to the edge of the main road, across the lane from the Conservative Club. The house had a full staff with maids, a butler, cook and gardener, etc. Mrs Ayres was left a widow who lived into her 90s and when she died around 1950 the property was pulled down. It was several years before the council developed the land but on 10 December 1964 a square brick-built library was opened on the site, and was later followed by a doctors' surgery and clinic, flats for the elderly and a community centre. Thankfully some of the mature trees from the garden remained.

A procession to celebrate the coronation of King Edward VII on 9 August 1902, with everybody in their Sunday best marching along the main road into Ripponden, following the Krumlin brass band. The spire in the distance belongs to Zion Chapel. There were events throughout Ripponden and Rishworth in celebration. This group had probably marched up the Rochdale road and down Dyson Lane and were now making their way back to Ripponden for a celebratory feed.

A group of Ripponden women who were performing in a concert at the Conservative Club in 1925. Standing left to right are Clara Wadsworth, Agnes Hamer, Dora Mellor, Adelaide Ackroyd and Doris Johnson while seated are Martha Kershaw and Connie Pearson.

A view of Ripponden, looking along the Ryburn Valley towards Rishworth. This shows the concentration of buildings in the village centre and the close proximity of the open countryside. Today there are one or two fewer mills and one or two more houses, but overall the scene is not much different.

The three-storey building left of centre here is the Chartists' or Foresters' Hall. No longer standing, this was a meeting hall where dances were also held to raise funds for various causes. The slightly lighter coloured building with the railings on the left was the Black Lion Inn and a couple of doors further along was the Canterbury Inn which closed in 1906. When the railway reached Ripponden the landlord of the Canterbury tried to attract customers by changing its name to the Railway. The cottages on the left behind the gas lamp were bequeathed to the church in 1914 and became the community centre. The two children are sitting on the doorstep of a one-time tobacconist's. The room above the archway was once the home of a church warden called Tommy Scott.

Kebroyd Silk Mills were destroyed by fire four times and this photograph was taken after the blaze of 6 November 1904, which left the mill a roofless shell although apparently a bible was discovered inside completely undamaged. Previous fires had occurred in 1868 and 1903, and after all three the mill was rebuilt. Lighting would have been powered by gas and plenty of oil was required to run the machinery efficiently, creating a very combustible environment. Plans to turn the mill into apartments in 2006 were also thwarted by fire.

Rishworth

The village of Rishworth stretches mainly along the Oldham Road, with some houses off Rishworth New Road. There is no centre to the village, as most of the properties on the main road are on the same side and stretch for a good mile. The surrounding moorland is very sparsely populated and generally used by hill farmers for sheep grazing. The better land in the river valley is used for dairy cattle, or raising stirks (young male cattle) for meat. This type of farming has been carried out in the area for centuries and before the cotton and woollen mills arrived on the scene many of the farmers would have supplemented their income by weaving cloth at home. Evidence of this can be seen today as a lot of the old properties have upstairs windows that stretch the full length of the property, allowing as much light as possible into the room for the weaver.

Like everywhere else in the valley, home weaving was superseded by mechanisation and five mills were opened in Rishworth, with several more in Ripponden easily reached by Rishworth folk looking for work. This opportunity took many of the small farmers into the mills.

The renowned Rishworth School was founded in the early 1700s to educate a small number of local children on a boarding school system. The Goat House was their lodging whilst the chapel that still stands at the top of Shaw Lane was the school house. Over the years the school has expanded with buildings now alongside the Oldham Road, and the original school, which was extended in the 1960s, is now the school chapel. Heathfield, the former home of the local landowners, the Wheelwright family, is now the preparatory school and the original Rishworth Mill, also owned by the school, now contains a swimming pool. Several of the village properties have been bought to house the staff and their families. The school became renowned over the world and many students boarded at the school.

With the M62 about five miles away from the village, the cities of Manchester, Leeds and Bradford are easily reached so Rishworth has expanded and quite a lot of farmland has been built on for new houses for commuters.

The organ in Rishworth Baptist Chapel was regarded as the best in the area. The organist would sit with his back to the congregation and the parson but still be able to see what was happening via the tilted mirror which can be seen here.

This is the main Oldham to Halifax road looking toward Rishworth. The photographer would nowadays have his back to the M62 junction and the motorway would be seen crossing the moors to the right of the photo. The building on the left is the Spa Inn; neither this or the building on the other side of the road exist today. However, the Spa Clough Reservoir is still there and little changed from when this photograph was taken. The house in the centre is also still there.

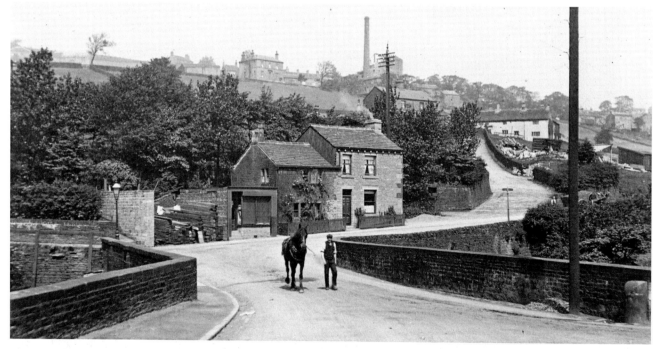

Slitheroe Bridge more or less marks the boundary between Rishworth and Ripponden. It crosses over the River Ryburn which then converges with the Booth Dean Clough just beyond the right side of the photo. The bridge has been widened since the photo, but the buildings at the far side of the bridge remain the same. The small square building next to the pile of timber has for many years been a shop and the houses are little changed. In the photograph the main road appears to continue up the hill toward the white house, but this is Dyson Lane and the road to Ripponden village runs behind the bush at the back of the telegraph pole. Just to the right of the pole is Dyson Lane sawmills, long gone, and probably the timber was stock for or from the mill. Top centre in the view is Dyson Lane Mill, again long gone.

This photograph of Slitheroe Bridge must have been taken after the trestle bridge to Rishworth Station had been demolished in the 1950s. It shows the River Ryburn as it meets the Booth Dean Clough.

This building, situated at the top end of Shaw Lane near its junction with Rishworth New Road, has been the chapel for Rishworth School since the 1920s. When it was built in 1725 it was the original school building. Local landowner, John Wheelwright, founded this school to educate the children of his tenants. The children, always more boys than girls, were lodged along with staff just around the corner in the Goathouse. This building was used as the school for over 100 years until the larger new school was built by the Oldham Road in 1828. Once the new building was occupied, the old school at one point served as a joiner's shop and a chapel for the people of Rishworth. It was extended in the early 1960s by a local building contractor who refitted the original gable window into the new gable.

A Rishworth Sunday school concert group photographed at the side of the Sunday school building which in those days backed on to fields which have since been built on. The terrace in the background is called Back Croft, unusual amongst all the other buildings in the village because it is brick built. The woman on the right of the group is Emily Holroyd. The Sunday school building has now gone and the open fields behind this group are now built on.

A group of Sunday school children photographed after performing the 'Pierette Princess' in 1929. This photo was taken on the grassed area outside the Sunday school building at Rishworth. The small building behind the group is the parson's vestry for the chapel, and the gable in the background is Back Croft. These kinds of concerts were a regular event at Christmas and Easter. The seven-year-old seated on the right is Jessie Holroyd.

The Naval Cadets were actually part of a Rishworth Baptist Chapel concert party. The house to the left of the photo is Little Hey. In the 1950s and 60s the owner of the house, Mr Thorman, allowed the Sunday school to take over his garden for the annual garden party. A tennis ball cricket match was held on his well-tended lawn and bottles of orange juice were sold for a few pennies from his caravan, while later there was a buffet tea back across the road in the Sunday school. On the ground where the photograph is taken, for a few years in the 1960s there was an annual 5th November bonfire (or the Saturday nearest to the 5th). So much wood was collected that this fire burnt for several days, with more fuel added daily until it was all used up.

Four junior members of the 1929 Rishworth Baptist concert party, photographed behind the Sunday school. The two taller girls are Irene Horsfall on the left with her sister Edna third from left.

Members of Rishworth Baptist Chapel in the mid 1930s. The Rev. Hirst, minister at the time, was only at Rishworth for a couple of years from 1936. Sunday school trips were an annual event and often involved a visit to the seaside, Morecambe being a favourite. I can also recall trips to Manchester Airport and Chester Zoo, with Glenway Coaches from Ripponden being the usual transport.

Standing left to right: Ethel Davies, Bryan Crawshaw, Elsie Basnett, Edgar Crawshaw, Edna and John Lumb, Joe Wadsworth, Leonard Basnett, Jessie Holroyd, Wallace Whiteley and Hilda Basnett.

Seated left to right: Mrs Evelyn Horsfall, Marrion Ramsbottom, May Leaver, Dorothy Ramsbottom, the Rev. Edwin Hirst, Emily Crawshaw, Emily Basnett, Alice Basnett and Mrs Joe Wadsworth.

Seated on the ground: Hubert Gee, John Wadsworth and Arthur Bennett.

Rishworth Baptist Chapel, on the right of the photograph, was built in 1803. The two houses on the left of the photograph were owned by the chapel, the nearest one being rented out and the other being the caretaker's house. Originally the Sunday school was based in these two houses until a hall was built behind the chapel in 1897. To the side and front of the chapel was a graveyard with some very elaborate memorials. A further cemetery is a couple of hundred yards away on the Rishworth New Road where there was also a small chapel and the manse where the parson lived. Over the years the attendances at the chapel dwindled and finances were not sufficient to keep the building in good order. Eventually it was bought and converted into a private dwelling.

Rishworth Sunday School was built in 1897 behind the Baptist Chapel on the Oldham Road. The building comprised a large hall with a stage at the far end, two small classrooms, one large classroom that could be opened up using folding doors, two kitchen rooms, one office and toilets each side of the main entrance. A dumb waiter gave access to a downstairs storeroom cum workshop where water was boiled for tea making. The building was well used for concerts by chapel members and visiting groups from other local chapels, jumble sales, whist drives and a lending library. Under the stage was a large tiled bath with tiled steps that was used for baptisms. The building was seriously affected with dry rot and woodworm and had to be demolished in the 1970s.

Local landowner Mr Wheelwright lays the foundation stone at Rishworth Church. The inscription on the stone reads 'In the faith of Jesus Christ, this stone was laid by J.R.H. Wheelwright on the 28th day of May 1927'. The builders used a local stone with a pinkish hue which adds a lot of character to the building. The stained glass window in the apple and pear design is dedicated to John Wheelwright, the founder of Rishworth School and the carvings in the church were carried out by Harry Percy Jackson, who was the son of a wood carver whose business was at Coley. He was not totally dedicated to the family business, however. In 1922 he went to the USA and became involved in the film industry, appearing as an extra in *The Sea Hawk* and *The life of Abraham Lincoln*. He returned to England three years later due to his father's illness. In 1926 he went to Canada, but returned for the same reason, this time staying. His son did the carving on the Bishop's Chair in the church.

This trestle bridge was built in 1880 to link Rishworth railway station with the main Halifax to Oldham road at Slitheroe. This was a massive construction built of timber with stone setts paving the roadway which was 20 feet wide. Goods in and out of the many mills in the area and especially coal to fire the boilers and provide the power made this size of bridge necessary to take the horse and motor transport that completed deliveries. Passenger services to Rishworth had ceased in 1929 and goods went no further than Ripponden by 1952, so this bridge was demolished in 1953. The concrete foundation blocks that supported the bridge are still in place.

Rishworth Cricket Club was formed in 1899. The club played its home games at Rishworth Hall, a narrow strip of land adjacent to the Rishworth School playing fields on the left-hand side of Rishworth New Road between the village and Commons. The ground was so narrow that boundaries parallel to the pitch counted two runs as opposed to the normal four. This was the case for quite a few clubs in the area. A neighbouring club, Stones, had markers on the walls to divide the short and longer boundaries and determine a two from a four. Rishworth played in the Halifax Amateur Cricket League, established in 1892. This was open to any club within the Halifax boundaries that could provide basic standards of ground, facilities, administration and finance. By 1907 there were 44 clubs involved but these began to decrease during the following years. From 1892 to 1922 a total of 158 teams had played at least one season in the league, a vast number of clubs, and this was not the only league in Halifax. In 1922 the Halifax Amateur Cricket League amalgamated with the Halifax and District League to form the Halifax and District Amateur Cricket Association. The Rishworth club was not reformed after the war and a council estate was built on the ground in the 60s. The club won the Collinson Cup in 1934 and were league winners in 1932.

Members of Rishworth Cricket Club, photographed in front of their pavilion at Rishworth Hall in 1923. Records do not show a trophy for that year. Back row left in the suit is Fred Holroyd and next to him is Hartley Greenwood, a local farmer. In the front row second from the left is Jimmy Galloway; next to him is Newton Holroyd, then there is Laurie Broadbent and then John Whiteley.

Rishworth Cricket Club, 1st XI, 1934.
Back row, left to right: Walter Schofield, Tom Morton, Harry Beaumont, Irvin Holroyd, unknown, Evelyn Horsfall, Stephen Schofield, Harry Lumb, Hammond Leeworthy, Wilf Hopkinson and Jimmy Holroyd.
Front row, left to right: unknown, Albert Jenkins, John Morton, Michael Wheelwright, Joe Leaver and Jimmy Galloway.

Rishworth Cricket Club, Halifax & District League Division 1 winners, 1932.
Back row, left to right: unknown, Tom Morton, Willie Taylor and Stephen Schofield.
Middle row, left to right: George Edgar Hurst, Jimmy Holroyd, Newton Holroyd, Geoffrey Mellor, John Morton, Laurie Broadbent, Charlie Wood, Wilf Hopkinson, Hartley Greenwood, John Whiteley and Percy Horsfall.
Front row, left to right: Evelyn Horsfall, Albert Jenkins, Major Greenwood, Edward Jenkins, Joe Leaver and Hammond Leeworthy.
Major Greenwood was a local farmer whose Christian name was actually Major.

Rishworth Football Club, pictured with the 1924 Challenge Cup. The photograph was taken in front of Rishworth Junior School on Godley Lane. The club's ground was on Rishworth New Road opposite Rishworth School's playing fields.

Rishworth Football Club 1925–26, showing off its silverware. Back row left is Hammond Leeworthy, sixth from left is Wilf Hopkinson and seventh is Fred Holroyd. The suited gent in the middle row left is John Holroyd and on the same row right is Albert Tweed. Some of the footballers are, middle row left Willie Normanton, third left Alec Mitchell, fourth Ted Drake, fifth John Morton. On the front row left is Tommy Bassnett, third left is Reynard Forbes, and on the right is Teddy Eastwood.

This is Rishworth National School's football team of 1924, photographed on the paved area of the playground in front of the school. The lad with the ball is possibly Douglas Galloway. The school was opened in 1874 and changed little until extensions started to be added in the mid 1960s. Even today the frontage of the original school can easily be made out. The building comprised three classrooms, an assembly hall that doubled as a dining hall, a kitchen and a house that was probably used by the head teacher originally but by the late 1950s was occupied by the caretaker and his family. In the early 1960s each child in the school would spend two years in each of the three classrooms. The first two with Mrs Telford, Standard 1 and 2 with Miss Maude and then 3 and 4 with the headmaster, Mr Crossley, who kept a couple of beehives in the garden at the back of the school. If any child was unfortunate enough to get stung he would remove the sting, wrap it up in a piece of paper and give it to them to take home. There was a kitchen facing the playground, but little cooking took place here as it was basically just a washing-up station. Instead, school lunches cooked in Ripponden would arrive in a little van, driven by Johnny Beverley the local cobbler and one time Ripponden mayor, half an hour before required, to be kept warm. Stones School was also on his delivery round. The only hot water in the school was in the kitchen so water monitors in the top class would leave lessons ten minutes early at lunch time to transport buckets of hot water to the three classrooms. The toilets were an outdoor affair with no roof. Extensions and alterations began in 1965 and the whole school, probably no more than 50 to 60 pupils, moved to Rishworth Baptist Sunday school until the work was completed. On Tuesdays 3.30 p.m., or 'loosing time' as it was called, always seemed to coincide with Ripponden greengrocer Frank Phillips serving customers from his van opposite the school. He would throw handfuls of monkey nuts on the grass at the side of the school and all the pupils would dive after them.

A view along the road through Booth Woods, with the photographer standing with his back towards Rishworth. The building in the background on the hill is a farmhouse and barn typical of the area. The land is generally too steep for crops so farming meant sheep, hens for food and eggs, a few milk cows, perhaps a few pigs and a few castrated young bulls, known locally as stirks, to be raised for meat.

Bogden Woods was a popular beauty spot visited by many families and couples on their Sunday outings, easily and quickly reached from Rishworth and Ripponden. The Bogden flows from the watershed of the Pennines, passes close to the small settlement of Parrock Nook, before joining the Ryburn. This all changed when the Ryburn Dam was built close to the junction of the two streams. The building of the dam took several years to complete, but the beauty of the area was spoilt as soon as work began on the dam. Wakefield Council planted thousands of trees round the new structure to cover the damage caused but these trees took years to mature and for many people this area would have been ruined. Eighty years on the trees and shrubs have matured and the area is once again a very pleasant place to visit.

Rishworth School by the Oldham road. This school building replaced the original in 1827. It contains classrooms, a dining room and boarding accommodation. At the left-hand end of the building was the headmaster's house, which in 1971 was converted into girls' accommodation. A house had been built for the Headmaster in what had been a vegetable garden out of view further to the left. Behind this frontage is a courtyard surrounded by further rooms. The school owned several properties in the village to house the staff. Two of these were opposite the school on the other side of the Booth Dean Clough, one a farm, the other a small cottage. A steel and wood bridge was built over the river to access these properties.

This extension to Rishworth School was built in the early 1930s on land next to the old building and the photograph was used on an advertising card from Harry Castle, slaters. The cards state that the roof was of Welsh blue slate and that the extension cost £23,000. Alumni of the school include the novelist Dr Frank King (who also wrote under the name Clive Conrad), the TV presenter John Noakes, and Theo Crutchley-Mack who in 2010 had a design for a 50 pence piece accepted by the Royal Mint. He won the coin in gold and £10,000 for the school.

An event at the Cunning Corner pub in the 1920s. The pub has since changed its name to the Old Boar and has gained a porch and lost a barn. The circle of musicians in the field is the Rishworth Band. In front of the pub can be seen a bus. The bus route from Halifax to Rishworth normally terminated at Rishworth New Road, where there was a shelter, although through the day the route was occasionally extended to run to the Cunning Corner or to the Commons. As seen here, the bus was parked outside the pub until time for the return journey to Halifax. At the Commons, which is a mile or so along Rishworth New Road, past Rishworth School's playing fields, the terminus had a shelter made from an old tram car.

Carverclough is a terrace of 12 houses built in the early 1900s and named after the small stream that flows under the road, more or less where the photographer is standing, and down the hill into the Booth Dean Clough. These are quite spacious cottages, each having two rooms downstairs, three up, a well-ventilated cellar and a coal cellar. They also had allotments in the back field although these were taken over by a local farmer until the 1960s when it was built on. The second house from the far end of the photograph was the village post office for many years. Originally the houses were numbered 1–12 Carverclough but they are now 240–262 Oldham Road.

THE DERBY, RISHWORTH MOORS, RYBURNDALE. RSH. 9.

The Derby Bar Hotel on Rishworth Moor is the last hostelry on the Yorkshire side of the border. In the days when this photograph was taken the hotel's view would have been open moorland, but the Booth Wood Reservoir has since been built just over the road. The opening of the M62 was responsible for a name change for the inn to Junction 21, which is just a couple of miles away. Today it is called The Turnpike. The inn was a popular excursion destination in the early years and offered 'choicest wines, spirits & cigars, good accommodation for cyclists, good stabling'. This was detailed on business postcards when A.G. Henley was the proprietor. It was also famous for its ham and eggs. Today the building bares little resemblance to how it looks in this view.

A terrace of houses at Turner Bottom which are actually larger than this photograph might suggest. The land behind this terrace drops away very sharply to the Booth Dean Clough so it was possible to build another terrace under the one that can be seen from the road, making four storeys in total. These underdwellings have long since been condemned as unfit for habitation as they are basically 50% underground and prone to damp. The building at the left was at one time a joiner's shop and the building in the centre, on the other side of the road, was the toilet block for the terrace. Also on the other side of the road, between the two trees is Godley Lane which leads to the Clothes Hill, an area for hanging washing.

An artist's impression of the Church of St John The Divine, Rishworth. Belying the traditional design, this was built in 1928; before then the nearest church was in Ripponden, as all the other local places of worship were chapels. A lych gate was added in 1938.

The road over Rishworth Moor passes over Lower Bridge, seen here with the two cars heading for the Lancashire border. The Booth Dean Clough here is little over a mile from its source and the stream joining it via the bridge is one of many to do so as it passes down the valley. A little further back along the road now stands the dam wall of the Booth Wood Dam, the most recent of the three dams in the Ryburn Valley, and also supplying water to Wakefield. There is a pipeline over the moors connecting this dam with Baitings, so that water can be transferred from one to the other. The shape of the valley is ideal for reservoir building as the steeper the valley sides, the easier and quicker it was to build the wall.

The road across Rishworth Moor. Today the M62 would be visible on the sky line and Junction 21 would be just around the corner, top left. In those days, once leaving Rishworth there would be very few properties or people to be seen until Denshaw was reached after about eight miles. Denshaw is in fact in Yorkshire but the road crosses into Lancashire before returning back over the border.

Rishworth and Ryburn Valley Prize Brass Band was formed in the 1860s and survived until the 1930s. In 1906 it won the Daily Graphic Challenge Cup Contest at Crystal Palace, London. The band used a practice hall at Slitheroe House, which is on the left-hand side of Stead Lane. A favourite activity for the band was to march from pub to pub, taking time out to have a smoke and a drink at each one. This earned the band the title 'The Beer and Baccy Boys'.

On Saturday, 7 April 1906, four men were travelling home to Oldham in a horse and trap when the horse was spooked by something and crashed through the wall and over the edge of the delph ('delph' being the local word for quarry). Three of the four were killed and so was the horse. The three who died were William Shaw, William Smithies and William Kenworthy. This quarry is close to the Turnpike Inn, or Derby Bar as it was called in those days.

Heathfield is situated at the junction of the Oldham Road and Mill Lane and was the home of the Wheelwright family. In 1950 the building was bought by Rishworth School to be used as a preparatory school for the senior school, which is about a quarter of a mile further along the road towards Ripponden. Behind the house is the oldest of the two Rishworth mills, famous in its day for cotton production. This was also bought by the school. Some of it was demolished whilst other bits were turned into extra space for the school, including a swimming pool. The newer mill was also originally a cotton mill but in later years became part of the Crossley Carpet Co. and has since been turned into apartments.

Rishworth War Memorial is in a small triangular garden at the junction of the Oldham Road and Rishworth New Road. It consists of a large piece of local Millstone Grit with two bronze plates displaying the names of the fallen. It was unveiled on 11 November 1923 by Brigadier-General Sir George Ayscough Armytage. The ten who did not return from the Great War are Maurice Ainley, Ernest Britton, Geoffrey E. Elliott, Albert Gledhill, Edger Gledhill, Leonard Hartley, Willian Henry Jenkins, Sam Parkinson, Leonard Smith and Selwyn Sykes. The second plate for the Second World War shows two names: Edward C Kingsford and James Reid. The two buildings that can be seen in the distance are Lower Hey to the right and Rishworth Junior and Infant School on Godley Lane to the left.

The Cunning Corner inn is about three quarters of a mile further along the Lancashire road from the village. This was originally a coaching inn, but would have had quite a lot of competition as they were plentiful along the route from Ripponden. In the 1840s it was called the Coach and Horses and by 1857 had become the headquarters of the Oddfellows order, taking The Oddfellows as its name. In recent times it has been named The Old Bore. In the 1870s a horse-drawn haulage business was operating from here run by John Holroyd. The No. 62 bus from Halifax to Rishworth occasionally went the extra distance to the 'Corner', as it was known locally.

Irvin Holroyd was born in Rishworth in 1890 and apart from serving in the trenches, and regular holidays to Morecambe, lived there until his death in 1984. He spent his working life at Rishworth Mill where he started as a 'half timer' at the age of 10. This involved a morning shift from 6 o'clock to noon at the mill and an afternoon at school. His main job as a child was as a 'piecener', which involved getting into moving machinery to tie any broken ends of cotton. This was a job that only children could do because of the limited space in the machinery. He was called up and served in the trenches of the Somme but trench foot and a gas attack meant that he was sent home, and for the rest of his life he could neither taste nor smell due to the gas and his legs below the knees were permanently cold. He lived with his wife, Sarah Emma, and his two children, Jessie and Albert, at the Chapel House next to the Baptist Chapel where he was caretaker for many years. In later life he was, for a couple of hours most days, to be seen sitting on a roadside bench smoking his pipe and watching the world go by.

Top left: This was one of a string of beacons set across the country to celebrate the silver jubilee of King George and Queen Mary. It was built on top of Pike End Hill by the Rishworth Urban District Council and was 26 feet in height. It was built from railway sleepers and set alight on 6 May 1935. The council worker in the photo is William Shepherd.

Top right: Fred Holroyd was younger brother to Irvin and elder brother to Newton and he led a very similar life to them. Born in the early 1890s, he began work at Rishworth Mill, but missed out on the 'half timer' situation as this was discontinued. After his time in the trenches he continued his working life at the mill, where he worked until his retirement. He married Annie Leaver and lived at Carverclough, Rishworth. They were married for more than 60 years and were very pleased to show off their telegram from the Queen. To supplement his income he kept hens on a flat plot of land beside the Booth Dean Clough. In later life his eyesight failed but he would still be found sitting on the bench with his brothers most days. He lived into his early 90s.

Left: A family photo taken probably in 1923 with four female members representing four generations. The child is Jessie Holroyd, born on 13 November 1922. Her mother stands to the right and her grandmother to the left, while Jessie is sitting on the knee of her great grandmother. All four were born, brought up, worked and died in Rishworth.